The Self-Completing Tree

William Kinsley
Montréal 2007

Dorothy Livesay

Selected Poems

The Self-Completing Tree

Porcepic Books
an imprint of

Beach Holme Publishing
Vancouver

This edition is published by Beach Holme Publishing, #226 — 2040
W. 12th Avenue, Vancouver, B.C. V6J 2G2. This is a Porcepic Book.

We acknowledge the financial
support of the Canada Council
for the Arts, the Government of
Canada through the Book Publishing
Industry Development Program
(BPIDP) and the assistance of the
Province of British Columbia
through the British Columbia Arts
Council for our publishing activities
and program.

THE CANADA COUNCIL | LE CONSEIL DES ARTS
FOR THE ARTS | DU CANADA
SINCE 1957 | DEPUIS 1957

Cover Art: "Elm Tree at Horton Landing" Alex Colville, 1965
Oil on masonite 47 7/8 x 35 7/8 Art Gallery of Ontario. Used with
permission.
Editor: Joy Gugeler
Cover design: Teresa Bubela
Production and Text design: Jen Hamilton
Author photo: Elaine Brière

Canadian Cataloguing in Publication Data

Livesay, Dorothy,
        The self-completing tree

        ISBN 0-88878-258-6

        I. Title
        PS8523.I84S4 1999   C811'.54   C86-091378-3
        PR9199.3.L58S4 1999

À mon âme-soeur du Québec, Madeleine Gagnon, poète.

I'll walk where my own nature would be leading:
It vexes me to choose another guide:
Where the grey flocks in ferny glens are feeding;
Where the wild wind blows on the mountain side.
                                    —Emily Brontë

Acknowledgements are due for poems previously published in journals, and in books published by Coach House Press, Fiddlehead Poetry Books & Goose Lane Editions, Ryerson Press and Press Porcépic, but over which I now have the copyright. Especially I owe thanks to those editors and critics who have been working on my papers: Lindsay Dorney, University of Waterloo, whose collection of essays, *Dorothy Livesay: The Public and Private Voice*, was first aired at a conference in 1983 and will be published in August 1986; Lee Briscoe Thompson, whose literary study, *Dorothy Livesay*, will appear in 1987, published by G.K. Hall of Boston in their Twayne World Authors series; and Sandra Hutchison, whose thesis, *Form and Vision in the Poetry of Dorothy Livesay* won her a PhD in 1986 at the University of Toronto. Their concern and love for my poetry has sustained me through this aging decade, as has the enthusiasm and reliability of my secretary, Marie Hardy.

Other books by Dorothy Livesay:

Green Pitcher, Macmillan of Canada, 1928
Signpost, Macmillan of Canada, 1932
Day and Night, Ryerson Press, 1944
Poems for People, Ryerson Press, 1947
Call My People Home, Ryerson Press, 1950
New Poems, Emblem Books, 1955
Selected Poems, Ryerson Press, 1957
The Colour of God's Face, Unitarian Church, Vancouver, 1964
The Unquiet Bed, Ryerson Press, 1967
The Documentaries, Ryerson Press, 1968
Plainsongs, Fiddlehead Poetry Books, 1969, 1971
Disasters of the Sun, Blackfish, 1971
Collected Poems: The Two Seasons, McGraw-Hill Ryerson, 1972
Nine Poems of Farewell, Black Moss, 1973
Winnipeg Childhood, Peguis Press, 1973
Ice Age, Press Porcépic, 1975
Right Hand Left Hand, Press Porcépic, 1977
The Woman I Am, Press Porcépic, 1977
The Raw Edges, Turnstone Press, 1981
The Phases of Love, Coach House Press, 1983
Feeling the Worlds, Fiddlehead Poetry Books & Goose Lane
    Editions, 1984

Contents:

- Wasteland = Alienation
- organized to bring about radical social change
- CCF.

—

THE POET LOVELY AS A TREE

by Linda Rogers

When Dorothy Livesay died in 1996 it was Victoria's freak Christmas blizzard that finally enshrouded her in silence; a writer who had battled a variety of stormy landscapes, including the snow of elderly dementia, for poetry. She was 85 years old. Surviving to this advanced age not only took courage, it also, as Helen Sontoff, scholar and life partner of novelist Jane Rule, said took "a lot of time." During that lifetime, Dorothy Livesay, "Dee" to her friends, adopted a combative rather than conciliatory attitude toward the encroaching twilight and physical frailty of her later years, steadfastly refusing to "go gentle into that good night."

Hers was a life spent assailing the "Mysterious Barricades" of Canadian poetry. But this musical reference to the flurried notes of Couperin's piece is not intended to evoke the street barricades of the French Revolution, but rather the image of French petticoats. A student of French language, culture and the language of revolution, her Sorbonne thesis was entitled, "Symbolism and the Metaphysical Tradition in Modern English Poetry" and articulates her study of the lyric and intellectual strains in contemporary verse. Here she studied the works of Ezra Pound, T.S. Eliot, the Sitwells, W.H. Auden, C.D. Lewis and Stephen Spender, acknowledging their influence on her own craft, even as her heart belonged to the revolutionaries.

Livesay kept her skirts about her as she marched into battle, a talent that garnered her an audience of feminists, historians and poets continually enthralled with her shape-changing women as described in this early unpublished poem:

WHERE IS IT?
Reader, if you are curious
To find in this book my proper self,
Warning! I, like the pepper pot,
Live each day on a different shelf.

The daughter of a journalist, the freethinking JFB Livesay, and a committed Christian activist, Florence Randal, she was also at the centre of domestic battles from an early age. Born in Winnipeg and growing up amid her parents' sexual and ideological household struggles meant peace was a fragile entity. This atmosphere created a neurotic tension for the young Livesay, but perhaps also became a source of creative material from which to draw later in her writing life. In spite of her parent's widely divergent points of view, Livesay had great respect for them individually and for the family as a social and cultural matrix. They taught her to take the moral and ideological high ground and to defend the rights of others as well as her own, brandishing the pen, always mightier than the sword.

Livesay lived through turbulent times: a depression, two world wars, struggles to achieve civil rights, a socialist upheaval and the rise of feminism. As a poet, she regarded none of these subjects taboo, damning bigotry, championing the right to talk freely about sex and challenging conservatism wherever she encountered it. In her poem "Picasso Sketching", she quotes the cubist painter as he shunts "his visions through the station,/ sets dynamite in open air, ignites creation." with the artists' rallying cry, "Il faut risquer tout!" Livesay selected the poems in *The Self-Completing Tree* largely because they tell the story of those risks and the joy of taking them.

Social revolution abroad and the draught and Depression at home took Livesay beyond the safe refuge of her middle class upbringing in Clarkson (now part of Mississauga, a suburb of Toronto) and beckoned models of revolutionary verse like Lorca and Neruda, who were willing to risk everything for change. In "Poetry Is Like Bread" she writes:

> *Poetry is like bread*
> Neruda said
> *It should be shared*
> by everyone

...

Our poem—everyone's—
must be   a message
for survival
Let it sound out clear
signpost and banner
plain talk:

NO MORE WAR

In "Lorca" she writes:

You dance. Explode
Unchallenged through the door
As bullets burst
Long deaths ago, your heart.

And song outsoars
The bomber's range
Serene with wind—
Manouevered cloud

> *Light flight and word*
> *The unassailed, the token!*

In addressing issues closer to home, Livesay herself adopted a tone that reflected the political rhetoric of the Canadian Left, which had its birthplace on the prairies, as she did. In "The Documentaries" section Livesay calls on the Canadian political conscience that took root in the religious fundamentalism of this biblical landscape, using her oratorical gifts in the service of social change. Many consider these poems inferior work, but much of her reputation rests on their righteous outrage and the musicality that informs their rhythmic progression. In "After Hiroshima," she justifies the naive idealism that led her, like the poet David, to her own confrontations with various contemporary Goliaths:

Not any more the visions and revelations:
Only in brief flashes is light received, good news.
Only a child's belief, rocked in a cradle of doubt,
Can prophesy our safety; illuminate our hope.

During the forties, the decade in which she was twice awarded the Governor General's medal for poetry for *Day and Night*, 1944, and *Poems for People*, 1947, her commitment to proletarian verse was cemented in the establishment of the journal *Contemporary Verse*, which she edited with Alan Crawley and others involved in the Vancouver Poetry Society. *CVII*, the little sister to this publication, established in the seventies, was another landmark in her life, and the life of the country, when it became a forum for feminist literature in English Canada.

In the section "Rites Of Passage" Livesay reveals the crucible of her feminism and explores the implications of sexual ambiguities and gender never losing reign of the erotic. In "Letter at Midnight" she is male and female, horse and rider, her sexuality, the matrix of poetry, a catalyst for struggle that extends beyond the bed into the political arena.

Behave to me with love:
I am one so self-encircled
Only a thoroughbred could hurdle
These tough hedges.

And there are traps beyond
Set by the cunning of hated hand

And crags to clamber
Only a bold surefooted beast
Would venture.

Behave to me with love:
I am a country field, untamed
Restless for rider.

Her portrait with Duncan McNair, her husband, also reveals two strong profiles, a world of difference and much sexual tension between them. Livesay married and had two children, Peter and Marcia, but, like her mother, her mind was often elsewhere. Her advocacy of women's rights led to exploration of other aspects of her sexuality in both heterosexual and homosexual relationships outside of marriage. This boldness made her an icon for feminists and post-feminists including language deconstructionists. Ironically their refusal to live inside the "male" parameters of language confused Livesay, a plain-speaking grandmother of feminist poetry. Though she was a feminist revered in both Canadian solitudes, she took issue with post-feminist writing that robbed her craft of precious words. Livesay was frustrated with New Poetry and its tenets arguing instead in "Without Benefit of Tape" that:

The real poems are being written in outports
on backwoods farms
in passageways where pantries still exist
or where geraniums
nail light to the window

She complained about the unintelligible scribble of academic poets while they likewise found Livesay's canon simplistic, her politics naive. Academic poets deplored her lack of subtlety. Others said Livesay "published too much" and her aesthetic was marred by the "shrillness of politics." Others still said she was not a good editor. Much of this was generated by competitiveness in a writing community, where the rewards for the craft were minimal. Even as the body of Canadian literature grew there was less and less public money to support their public lives. Dee fought for the professional rights of her colleagues and hoped for, but didn't depend on, the admiration of those whose rights she championed.

In the end she turned to her colleagues and friends, many with whom she also took issue on and off the page. Several of Livesay's poems are conversations with other poets in which questions are raised and answered in poetic dialogue; writers like P.K. Page, Emily Dickinson, Milton Acorn, Seymour Mayne and Phyllis Webb. "All the people I have known intimately, loving or hating, are here." she wrote in the forward

to her *Collected Poems* in 1972. "They have acted as catalysts."
In "Phyllis, Reading Her Poems" she writes:

> A juggler, she pulls out cards
> anonymous thoughts
> and throws them five at a time
> into the air

Her "Pear Tree" bears comparison with P.K. Page's "Deaf
Mute in the Pear Tree":

> Lucky this pear tree hears
>   if anything
> small bird cries percolating
>   through downwhite foam
> and children chugging on the chains
>   of sound
> practising language
> Lucky this pear tree seeped in sun
> shivering the air
>   in her white
>   doldrums
> taps with her roots
>   the worm's kingdom.

The two poets had a long and public history of disagreement:
one reasoned and brilliant, the other rough and passionate,
but there were concurrences. The pear tree for both is a place
of perfection and primal wisdom, a place where love lives in
the branches and bears fruit. The two wrestled publicly and
privately only to find resolution in Livesay's phrase and Page's
poem, printed in Livesay's memorial program, "But We Will
Rhyme in Heaven." Page wrote:

> The moment we meet
> tangles and snares spring up
> on the asphalt street,
>
> ...

rarefied air
where rancour is blown away
and remedial stars appear
and Venus is kissing the moon
as the Spanish say.

Throughout this volume Livesay evokes not only the pear tree, or the self-completing tree, but indeed the mythological Garden in full: its Biblical imagery; innocence corrupted by experience; its energy associated with children; and her own childhood garden both wild and tamed. In a 1987 broadside of her poem "Bellhouse Bay," she writes on pink paper with silver sketches of birds and fish and a moon that:

shone in the waters of the bay
so serene
one could believe in
an ongoing universe

...

This is not paradise
dear adam dear eve
but it is a rung on the ladder
upwards
towards a possible
breathtaking landscape

The garden is also profoundly linked to the notion of renewal, constant in Livesay's poetry, especially as darkness closed in near the end of her life. "'Geranus....Crane" in the title section of this volume introduces the phoenix as archetype, a pervasive figure in her work. It also gives us her recurring geranium, a flower which, even indoors, struggles toward the window and the light.

A wild witch girl she seems
yellow and dried and dead
but let her once touch down again
        (in earthen pot or flower plot)

geranium is phoenix still
        (an earthbound bird)
she fires that mould
          cranes up her neck
to steal the final word.

In the love poems of middle age in the section "The Unquiet
Bed," she recalls Africa where she went to teach for UNESCO
in 1959, a trip to the equator, her middle age, the middle
of the world. Here, in "Sorcery", the last frantic flowering of
sexual recreation is evident in every ripening fruit if also in
the creeping malignancies of mildew and death.

My breasts are withered gourds
my skin all over   stiffens
shrinks—the pubic hair
bristles to an itch

Not to be touched and swept
by your arm's force
gives me the ague
turns me into witch

O engineer of spring!
magic   magic me
out of insanity
from scarecrow into girl again
then dance me   toss me
catch!

In a recent lecture, writer Frank McCourt described the
progress of a life in art from fear to freedom, the two Fs at
opposite ends of our lives. Livesay's journey was unique in
that her turbulent but blessed beginnings allowed her to
move from freedom to freedom, gathering the fearful others
with her poetic rhetoric. Dorothy moved from the restless
garden of her childhood, where the swing from which she and
her sister Sophie shared their first view of the wilderness
beyond the flower beds and fences, to previously unclaimed

territories of the heart and mind. The tree that supported that swing still stands in this collection. Congruent with the affirmation her name proclaimed, Live/say, she lived to shout her own epitaph in the poem "Signature:

I dream of the next step
On into time—
Casting off skin,
Bones, veins and eyes,
Flower without root,
Dancer without feet—
Gone in a cone of spiralled air,
And I only wind
Sucked into the sun's fire!

The prairie gave breath; I grew and died:
Alive on this air these lives abide.

The Self-Completing Tree

This is the selection of poems that I would like to be remembered by. Rather than being strictly chronological, it is wrapped around certain themes that I see recurring throughout the years. I begin with poems about childhood, my own, my children's, other people's. From there the world widens, the acolyte is initiated through love. But is love the only gateway to maturity?

Poverty, racism and war have dominated my thinking and my emotions. As a social worker during the Depression, witnessing breadlines, riots, police brutality and the mass movements of the unemployed, my feelings were diverted from their primitive urgings – the desire for power, whatever the cost. Now, as powerful governments ignore the black harvest conferred on us by the disaster of Hiroshima and fail to consider the welfare of the environment over economic gain, my poetry remains an expression of my most passionate concerns: the danger of nuclear war, the plight of women politically and socially, the mistreatment of children, and the need for improved health and dietary standards in the third world.

Whether a leap is possible, a miracle of changed feeling, changed thinking – that is the theme of many of these poems.

Zambia: The Land

i

Implacable woman
the land reclines: dusty deaf
heart of stillness   mummified stillness
black

Sun rages   month on month
and men light fires   make branches totter
for fertile ash

But suddenly in November
a bird's voice fountains
thunder rants
rains tantrum
demanding   demanding

In a green swing upwards
the soil yields—
                    the land is dancing

ii

The still trees in late afternoon
are nameless elements
like elms they soar
like mushrooms wreathe the sky
At night they burst out suddenly
and fructify
with ripe moon-silvered fruit,
parade in columns
towards blue stars:
until the wild cicada shrills
telling the world their names.

Rooted strong on a hillside
or as a gnarled shadow
on windswept fields
the wild fig tree's
dry leaves
whistle November:
but on the sheltered side
fat leaves, bursting
declare April

And when the fruit forms clusters
and shoots dark red fingers
at the lusty sun
is it summer or winter?

Happy the self-completing tree
that brews, in secret,
its own seasons...

O wild fig tree
you dance in fire and ashes
over world's mouth
dance

The Difference

Your way of loving is too slow for me.
For you, I think, must know a tree by heart
Four seasons through, and note each single leaf
With microscopic glance before it falls—
And after watching soberly the turn
Of autumn into winter and the slow
Awakening again, the rise of sap—
Then only will you cry: "I love this tree!"

As if the beauty of the thing could be
Made lovelier or marred by any mood
Of wind, or by the sun's caprice; as if
All beauty had not sprung up with the seed —
With such slow ways you find no time to love
A falling flame, a flower's brevity.

Interval With Fire

Before I began to burn
with new found fire
this wintry summer had blown
had flown over.

Before I made the discovery
staked the claim
and stood at the rock's end
crying a name

stood arrested
on the alpine meadow
in amber light
flowing like honey—

before realization
of the total wonder
winter spoke
clouds massed in thunder.

I lifted my pack
turned to rock's shadow
closing my eyes
from the amber meadow.

Where storm swung down
to chasms again
I weighed my way
in the chill rain.
                    *
Now in the valley
past fisted cedars
black bog   lecherous arms
of devil's club

safe over burnt-out ledges
knee deep in slash
(the whited sepulchres
of our devotion)

safe at the level of
hitch-hike settlements
overflow from
a city's coldness

where the old man broods
on his apple tree   bitten
brown with evil
by the moth's bulldozer

and the old woman gathers
sour blackberries
from a wet season
a sodden September—

safe, but unsure
(back in the common place)
that there had ever been
an amazement

upon my eyes   a blast
of energy electrifying
my mind   a morning
when the heart blossomed—

(for the time of every day
is the time of misgiving:
in the habit of living
begins disbelief.)

So safe, but unsure
in the wet glitter of blessing
showered from a cherry-tree
shaken in September—

the sky tuned
and the rain shoved over:
I felt an arresting hand
held on the shoulder.

Sun called and controlled me
his shadow shared me
I rose to the mountains
where fire is no stranger

His day is now mine
an entering river
his blaze in my blood
flowing forever.

Unwritten Letter

The wind has torn your embroidered apples
From their boughs
And flung them on the ground:
The rain has filled your water-barrels
Full to overflowing,
Made channels through your beds,
And spattered all the shining window-panes
You loved to keep so clean.
Sun, too, has done his damage:
The goldenglow is short and shrivelled up,
The purple asters fade, and look forlorn,
And dahlias drop their petals
One by one,
And when the evening comes
Look for your watering-pot.
There is no happiness in your garden now—
Even the trees feel it.

All the neighbors are saying
They would like to see you again;
And I wish secretly
To meet you suddenly
Walking through your long, lonely avenue of elms.

Survival Kit — Bluff Park

Daffodils in spring
        shoot up joyous
on the edge of summer
        edge of the land
fringe of the sea
wild rose clambers
        amongst prickly gorse
gift of the English pioneers
mauve Scotch thistles
        maintain dominion
amongst bent-over grasses
        where protection lies
for the mountain lily
        white prototype
of Ontario's yellow dog-tooth violet.
Here Oregon grape   St. John's wort
white marguerites
find shelter beside rose campion
hugging the burnt grass cliffs.
These all   all survive
amongst fir   jackpine   maple
and the mothering arbutus
with its twining arms

Even after our blackened bones are buried
and the planet's face
is turned to stone
these memories of you and me
will thrive   survive
for, nameless, out of the crevices
these seeds will spring again
opening their rainbow colours
to the sun
to celebrate
all we have done
and undone.

Ballet

Each presentation
in front of the door-window
is a dance   with wind   rain   sun
scarlet geraniums curtseying
deference paid to the yellow rose
slowly revealing secrets

Towhees descend
morning   noon   night
to seek crumbs of home-baked bread
The father hones in   first
then birdlings   two   dark brown
stumble under railing
come for their lesson

As he nibbles at bread
they open their bills
and squeak
He darts for a piece of the white stuff
and stuffs it into
the near one's beak
But what about me?
whistles the other
In a trice he returns
pushes a speck
into the open beak

they hop about
dizzily
just beginning to know
how to eat
sleep   wake   search
find food where   there
somewhere

It has gone on for
millions of years
and who are we
with our absurd language
sleeping   waking   searching
to ask for a crumb of notice
from those upstairs?

Imminent Alert

Snow white
    foam on lighthouse rock
      clumsily   receding   recession
Snowwhite
    thick cluster of gulls
    studding the rock
    peaceful possession
aloft   upheld   by air
snowhite head
    bald eagle

Then salmon leap
    flash silver
shrill screams of gulls
thin treble of eagles
    dash under
what was a dance
is POUNCE!

Finches

Nonsense   I say to friends
They do not hear us
their ears are tuned
only to bird talk   close
family signallings
Even the crow or raven
causes no fluttering
least of all the ferry horn
or my door opening   closing

They live through their eyes
record hawk shadows hovering
watch from high   afar
in the arbutus trees
My comings and goings
my bread scattering
are peripheral

Our eyes stare blind
ears deaf
to the small sounds a child makes
or to our love's unuttered
song

Inter Rim

Today
I have come to terms
with books on the shelf
dishes in the cupboard
radio talk
and outside
the sea's changes
gull's gawk
(how they cluck cluck
softly in the morning
calling me to come out
and talk)

Today
I do not need
you   lover
nor you   friend
nor family
I can be
object against objects
sea against rock
clouds observing gulls
crab struggling
on sand

Today I intermingle
am host
to virgin or christ
or holy ghost
centred in crying
or laughing
loving
or dying

Today
I am tomorrow
and yesterday—
that song sparrow's lilt
on the old fence post—
Today
I am song itself

Celebrant

I move with the feeling of dying
of wind crinkling green leaves
into brown
of white petals falling
blown hither and thither
of weeds shrinking back
into loam
and the last song sparrow
singing hello to the rain

Farewell summer
Welcome winter!
vine maples splashing their blood
on the hillsides
sumac candles
profiles of peace   royal
red-purple—
eagles' shrill cry in the night

To die is to create renewal:
this crocus bulb pulsing
in my cradling hand.

Winter Solstice

Early morning: skirts of fog sweep in   hang over rumpled sea
till clouds explode   loosening their white dancers
from window's view nothing is there: only whiteness
only swirling snow

Inside: beside the fire we nod and drowse. An hour?
No, two. Then there is light:
a hidden sun pierces the curtain
fog vanishes   snow lies prone
spreadeagled over the garden grass

Below the cliff a darkening sea emerges
rippling   sinuous   slow

We wait. We listen half expecting
not ready for the song
that bubbles round the lighthouse rock.
Sea lions are here!   talking again
no male bark
but female chuckle   soft
yet strong with joy
bells within shells

We window watch: entranced
he steams up   close
and now he has her pinned
rocking her till the curling waves
seal them in   locked in a triangle
heads together clipped
their movements underwater based

And are there others   farther out
repeating these same calls?
We stand   amazed

rocked in our own embrace
then fling ourselves upon the couch
and beat that rhythm in our heaving cries

Postcard Mountains

We see them
and never see behind them
how flat they are
static
immobile   immoveable
cold   calculating
inhuman

O the flat platitudes
of the camera!

But we live here
in the valley
and they have become brothers
friends
enemies
frustrated lovers
This one looms ahead
of that one
That one
takes a great sloping stride
into a further range
beyond believing

At dusk
they seem to be shrouded
sleeping
body upon body
in relaxed curves
Yet now
somewhere on the west side
of the ranges

sun has set
and even in their sleeping
our mountains bristle
black silhouettes
soaring above
moon-white valleys

Even in their sleeping
we feel them ready to march
alert   awaiting the signal
Even in our sleeping
you and I and all our loves
dream of mountains
scaled   conquered   cherished
still stalwart
keeping guard
over this planet
even though dust of us
has vanished   perished

Erindale:
Hammond's Wood Revisited

"Paddle into the stream"—
numbing cold spring water
we lift the flat ones
slates of shale
heave them onto the bank
"Now you two girls
carry them carefully
into the boot of the car
higher and higher.
There, that'll do
All set? Climb in!"
And back with a heave and a ho
to build our rose garden at Woodlot.

It wasn't the heaving of the stones
or the spring day's heat
the fluttering green curl of poplar leaves
white grace of birches
It wasn't the drinking trough
at the side of the mud road
below the hill
where horse and buggy come by
even now   to drink
It was rather
the going into the wood
sandalled feet crushing the leaves
the going into bush   a shadowed slope
where in crannies
trailing arbutus trembled   tiny bells
and mauve hepatica   cup to the sun
and bloodroot   cream petalled star
pushing up from its red heart—
Last, in a sunny glade
trilliums! And father
now with spade

digging up the rare
pink ones   red ones
for his own woodland garden.

All these now
still blooming in May
fifty years after.

The Superiority of Flight

My unmated unmothering   old gull
Dinah
dives from the   roof
for the crusts I throw
utters a squawk   squawk   squawk
of thanks
and is off
sheer flight
into the sunset's
incoming tide

My lone gull
skims   keels   wheels
whirls onto sea's
heavy breast
needs no companion
makes her own self
      of herself   her wings
a home
      a nest.

September Equinox

Once morning mist
is pierced
by the sun's blades
and clouds wind-puffed away
these red-hot blades are
far more fierce
than any July's noon day

My cranky ankles   knees
melt in the blaze
and I am again
young naked girl
lulled on a bed of leaves

Unmusical Bird (blue heron)

His irritable hoarse
coughing cry
contradicts the slow   sure
heavy flight
weighted with wisdom
plumbed calm

Seeing him
alighting alone
as fisherman
in our small bay
we wonder how long
the hunters will let him
live on

Eve

Beside the highway
at the motel door
     it roots
the last survivor of a pioneer
     orchard
miraculously   still
     bearing.

A thud   another apple falls
     I stoop and O
that scent gnarled ciderish
     with sun in it
that woody pulp
     for teeth and tongue
     to bite and curl around
that spurting juice
     earth-sweet!

In fifty seconds, fifty summers sweep
     and shake me—
I am alive! can stand
     up   still
hoarding this apple
     in my hand.

'Geranus' .... Crane

Geranium
is like no other bird
    (turned plant)
its blossom scent
not sweet   hysterical
but acrid   herbal   healing
    (flying home)
and when it's rounded out the menstrual cycle
in a red blossoming
and needs a menopause
the plant   (the bird)
can be pulled up   and hung
dry on the rafters all the winter long.

A wild witch girl she seems
yellow and dried and dead
but let her once touch down again
    (in earthen pot or flower plot)
geranium is phoenix still
      (an earthbound bird)
she fires that mould
        cranes up her neck
to steal the final word.

Pear Tree

Lucky this pear tree has no ears
can grow and glow in whiteness
                      sunlightness
all undisturbed
                by snarling horns
                    unmuffled hooting cars
                        machine-powered lawn-
                          mower pushers
                            and machine-
                              saws shrieking into wood

Lucky this pear tree hears
                if anything
small bird cries percolating
                  through downwhite foam
and children chugging on the chains
                          of sound
practising language
Lucky this pear tree seeped in sun
shivering the air
                in her white
                        doldrums
taps with her roots
                the worms' kingdom.

Second Coming

What unwithering
                    is this?
        the gnarled tree un-
                    knotting itself?
White in autumn
                    the dogwood blossoms—
against red rowan
                    is green and white
                        coming   be
                            coming.

On Looking into Henry Moore

                    i

Sun   stun me   sustain me
turn me to stone:
Stone   goad me   gall me
urge me to run.

When I have found
passivity in fire
and fire in stone
female and male
I'll rise alone
self-extending and self-known.

                    ii

The message of the tree is this:
aloneness is the only bliss
Self-adoration is not in it
(Narcissus tried, but could not win it)

Rather, to extend the root
tombwards, be at home with death

But in the upper branches know
a green eternity of fire and snow.

iii

The fire in the farthest hills
is where I'd burn myself to bone:
clad in the armour of the sun
I'd stand anew alone

Take off this flesh   this hasty dress
prepare my half-self for myself:
one unit   as a tree or stone
woman in man   and man in womb.

Gloria

Whatever humans have dreamed of
        shall come to pass
the child is father to the man
the girl sees beyond   the woman
towards a thousand dancing children
black and white
        shall walk arm in arm
unarmed unharmed
chanting the song of the leaf
        the song of the bird
        the song of this little finger
these hands
and the tears of these eyes

O give us the peace of granite
        walking at snail's pace
frail as a butterfly's wing but
        fanning out into
ocean's architecture
and all the sky's inhabitants
clouds   stars in their legions
        swinging into
their ordained stations

The Childhoods

Strange how, as one grows older, scenes from one's life recur more and more dramatically.

Watching the rhythm of my own childhood repeated in the childhoods of my children and grandchildren, I've seen a fascinating counterpoint emerge. Instead of writing these poems I would have liked to have been a film maker, flashing the camera from one generation to another. The very thought is exciting.

I

Green Rain

I remember long veils of green rain
Feathered like the shawl of my grandmother—
Green from the half-green of the spring trees
Waving in the valley.

I remember the road
Like the one which leads to my grandmother's house,
A warm house, with green carpets,
Geraniums, a trilling canary
And shining horse-hair chairs;
And the silence, full of the rain's falling
Was like my grandmother's parlour
Alive with herself and her voice, rising and falling—
Rain and wind intermingled.

I remember on that day
I was thinking only of my love
And of my love's house.
But now I remember the day
As I remember my grandmother.
I remember the rain as the feathery fringe of her shawl.

Wilderness Stone

I dreamed that I dwelt in a house
On the edge of a field
With a fire for warmth
And a roof for shield.

But when I awoke I saw
There was nothing at all
But rain for my roof
And wind for my wall.

Serenade For Strings

i

At nine from behind the door
The tap tapping
Is furtive, insistent:
Recurrent, imperative
The I AM crying
Exhorting, compelling.

At eleven louder!
Wilderness shaking
Boulders uprolling
Mountains creating

And deep in the cavern
No longer the hammer
Faintly insistent
No longer the pickaxe
Desperate to save us
But minute by minute
The terrible knocking
God at the threshold!
Knocking down darkness
Battering daylight.

ii

O green field
O sun soaked
On lavish emerald
Blade and sharp bud piercing
O green field
Cover and possess me
Shield me in brightness now
From the knocking
The terrible knocking ....

iii

Again ... Again ... O again.
Midnight. A new day.
Day of days
Night of nights
Lord of lords.

Good lord deliver us
Deliver us of the new lord
Too proud for prison
Too urgent for the grave ...
Deliver us, deliver us.

> *O God the knocking*
> *The knocking attacking*
> *No breath to fight it*
> *No thought to bridge it*
> *Bare body wracked and writhing*
> *Hammered and hollowed*
> *To airless heaving.*

iv

The clock now. Morning.
Morning come creeping
Scrublady slishing
And sloshing the waxway
And crying O world
Come clean
Clean for the newborn
The sun soon rising ...

Rising and soaring
On into high gear ...
Sudden knowledge!
Easy speedway

Open country
Hills low-flying

Birds up-brooding
Clouds caressing
A burning noon-day ...

Now double wing-beat
Breasting body
Till cloudways open
Heaven trembles:
>   And blinding
>   searing
>   terrifying
>   cry!

The final bolt has fallen.
The firmament is riven.

v

Now it is done.
Relax. Release.
And here, behold your handiwork:
Behold — a man!

The Mother

She cannot walk alone. Must set her pace
To the slow count of grasses, butterflies,
To puppy's leap, the new bulldozer's wheeze
To Chinese fishman, balancing his pole.

She cannot think alone. Words must be
Poised to the smaller scope, immediates
Of wagon's broken wheel, a battered knee,
The sun's high promise for a day of play.

And when the active hours are gone, it's still
Her lot to busily bestir herself
With knots and nooses, all the slough and slips
Of day. When evening's seal is set she must

Have chosen here to stay. To sit, to hear
The day's confessions eased from tired tongue,
To soothe the small lids down to drowsiness
Till childhood sleep perfumes the darkened room.

Children's Camp

Call it safety—
That cool island where
No headlines glare
No rumour of the world
Disturbs the ear;
Boys' arms and legs
Are fancy-free
To spin like catherine wheels
Through hours of play
Until, at night
With campfire at the throat
Their hearts sing out, sing out
They chant their way and float
To airy sleep.

Though gongs awaken
Summer is a season of high bells
Rung in the skies, and shaken
Through green leaves calling out a dance,
Sun's baton striking time:
So bells ring out all day!
But clock's invisible
And day moves into week
Unchained by calendar or season;
Hours need no rhyme
And summer needs no reason.

Call it safety
That island where
No motors hum
No planes drone
No bombs loom—
Here childhood is miraged,
Anchored in dream
A cordon against sound.

Call it safety, where
Under the tall star
And the cedar bough
A dream takes form.

Abracadabra

In the wicked afternoon
When the witch is there
When night's downsnare
Swoops like a loon
Strafing the air
In the wicked afternoon

In the witty time of day
When the mind's at play
The cat's at call
The guitar off the wall
Wind holds sway
In the witty time of day

Then the witch will walk
Full of witty talk
And the cat will stalk
Tail high as a cock

The guitar in the room
Will fuss and fume
Strumming at the tune
For a wicked afternoon
And out in the park
Wind will unfrock
The autumn trees
And falling leaves
Shiver with shock.

And time with his
Weaving, wailing horn

Shivers my timbers
Shatters my corn:
Little boy blue
Blows a blue tune
On a wicked afternoon.

Blue Wind

Spirit of wind
blue skirt against blue-green grass
hair fair
straw-coloured
straight and prim
a coif   for skyblue eyes
staring amazed
at the wild
woods   fields
folding hills
ever yielding
ever flowering
earth

Spirit of wind
granddaughter
moving undaunted
round the bend
into the frightening
tight-drawn highways

Against these,
blow and burn!
contrive to comprehend
survive to sway
to the will of the wind.

Small Fry

Their cries
Rise and recede
As hills by train
Heave huge and blot the sky
Shrill with demand
Then fall and fan
Into the muted ripples of a plain.

Their talk
Is bird brief, irresponsible
The answer asked
Not waited for
And the word punched
Back like a volley ball.

Their song is man's
Own early voice
Heart free and eased
Throat seized
With tremors of light
Sun's scale from branch to branch
Storming delight.

The High

On the sand
he whirled for five
six   seven   eight
ten minutes
oblivious
to calling come

turning alone
he whirled, a small
black cone
at the water's edge

"I was just trying to see
if a man really could take off
like a plane.
You don't believe it, do you, Gran?"

I believe!   I believe!

Isolate

To find direction
the only child creates a web of action

pulling them in, to play
new, unknown games
making herself a centre

And everyday
she thinks of a new way
for charming them: some twist
to *Hide and Seek* they'd never thought of
some long manoeuvre of the map
of *Hoist Your Sails*.
And finishes, on Saturdays
holding them all intent
in half-pint chairs on the dish-towel lawn
chalking sums on a child's blackboard.

Then thunder breaks:
across the street
the firebell clangs
and the great grey horses stamp
in a burst of doors
deafen the asphalt with their hooves.
Games fall apart
as children fly like sparks
with whoops and shouts into the charging street.

She stands alone at the gate:
games fall apart.

On Holding A Baby

Small sad bundle of new flesh and bone
you peer at us from a stranger place,
fasten your eyes on objects motionless
yet dazzling bright

As if in that dark cave
where you lay girdled in life's structured bands
you knew the hush   savored the sure heart beat
diastole   systole
lulled in the ebb and flow
and now, being plunged
into fierce cross-currents
light   dark   action   rest
love   hate,
your wonderment exceeds your fear
and curiosity overcomes
the vastness of the myth
till, from an overdose of sense impressions,
clutch of hunger   gripe of thirst,
you seek and are satisfied
and quench the eyes' blue fountains
in a drift of sleep.

If there are guardians round you
they do not reveal
how ably you'll take hold of pain
and shake it off
and twist the corkscrew in your heart
and turn and laugh again.

Five Months Young

He's the sun
of man
he's trailing
clouds
falling into
flower gardens

If we could offer anything
to the indifferent gods
against our destruction of
forest   field
river   lake
ocean's salty hemisphere
the Arctic's icy shape
it would be this small
cradled baby
who cannot speak
whose blue eyes illumine
every text
whose smile
invites the universe
to be plain human

II

Signature

Born by a whim
This time
On a blowing plain
I am as wind
Playing high sky
With a name—
Winnipeg!

So prairie gave breath:
Child head, anemone
Raised from winter grass
Pushing the mauve-veined cup
Upward to world all sky
Peopled with cloud.

Ages before
These violet veins
Fingered their mauve
Through England's green;
These crocus eyes
Glowed in stone
Or a poplar row
Sturdy with Normandy;
Or a sea-wall—
War's peep-hole.

And longer than summers
Of conquering blood

Were my feet running
In a Roman wood
And my hair bound
In a vestal hood.

Stretched on the solitary sand
Of Egypt, I lay asunder:
Till the lover came,
The flowering night
Shaped me a name
And the earth shook under.

Now when I waken here
Earthbound
Strapped to the sound
Of a Winnipeg wind;
I dream of the next step
On into time—
Casting off skin,
Bones, veins and eyes,
Flower without root,
Dancer without feet—
Gone in a cone of spiralled air,
And I only wind
Sucked to the sun's fire!

The prairie gave breath; I grew and died:
Alive on this air these lives abide.

Teachers

Teachers who taught
                me
the delicacy of French
the symmetry of
                equations
the incredible
     subtlety
of English variations
teachers who taught me

I meet you now
you vigorous women
in your seventies
and eighties
and it's I who marvel
that you kept
your gaze fixed
on mankind's magical
                strivings
and never shrugged me off
as a poor child
frumpily dressed
obviously not
belonging in the
establishment
never shrugged me off
as a hopeless
     non-conformist
but somehow loved
my twisted awkward frame
my freckled vision
somehow saw
how I might one day strike outward
flaying the waters
to be a person

Canadiana

My grandmother's house in Winnipeg
stood opposite Luxton School
yellow-brick
solid as Victoria herself.
The roaring children
terrified my tremulous
protected childhood
and I came home from class
with nits in my hair
and a vision of small brutes
throwing tin cans
shouting "Yid! Yid!"
at my mother's best friend's
Jewish son.

Today in my old years
protected by knowledge
I take up lodgings in Edmonton
opposite a red brick school
solid   Victorian
with battlemented turret.
On the sloping lawns
a sign
KEEP OFF THE GRASS
Luckily they do not
but roll on it
play cowboys   Indians
and when the first snow falls
softly   softly
cloaking the school yard
they leap and slide
on these small slopes—
the closest they may ever come
to flying.

The Children's Letters

They are my secret food
consumed in the most hushed corners
of my room
when no one's looking
I hold them up to sunlight
at the window
to see aright
to hear behind the spindly words
a child's tentative
                    first footsteps
a small voice stuttering
                    at the sky
"bird ... bird ..."

Whether these be
my children or my grandchildren
they're ghostly visitors
food of a solitary kind—
they leap on shafts of sunlight
through the mind's
shutters.

And Even Now

When I was a child,
Lying in bed on a summer evening,
The wind was a tall sweet woman
Standing beside my window.
She came whenever my mind was quiet.

But on other nights
I was tossed about in fear and agony
Because of goblins poking at the blind,
And fearful faces underneath my bed.
We played a horrible game of hide-and-seek
With Sleep the far-off, treacherous goal.

And even now, stumbling about in the dark,
I wonder, Who was it that touched me?—
What thing laughed?

Waking in the Dark

Whenever I see him
in mind's eye
I see him light-haired and laughing
running in a green field

But day comes
radio is turned on
newspaper is insinuated
under the door
and there   between comic strips
ads   and girdled girls
black words mushroom:

> It's going to take a hundred years
> > the experts say
> to finish this genocide
> a hundred years to annihilate a people
> to bitter the ricefields with blood
> dry Delta's water into salt—
> a hundred years
> > so our grandchildren growing up
> > and their children
> will be humans who feel no pity
> > for the green earth
> and who look upon procreation
> > with indifference

When I see my grandchild running
in a game of football
his helmet is empty
in his right arm
he carries his head.

The Halloweens

i

The children have taken my bell!
just a small brass bell
from India
hung on the door lintel
to signal
some friend's arrival
      (as if they had taken a book
       or some poems
        and thrown them into the ditch)
the children have taken my bell

ii

I remember being twelve years old
wearing a black mask
over my eyes
a witch's cloak
over my shoulders
walking along Bloor St. with my sister
crying in the grocers' doorways
"Shell out! Shell out!
Halloween apples!"

iii

I remember the hard darkness
of teenage Halloween parties
when my mother dressed me
in an authentic Ukrainian costume
(borrowed from a dancer)
to be greeted with:
"The girls are all dressed as ghosts—
wouldn't you like a sheet?"
And shamefully

I let them re-dress me
in a sheet.

Late   late
cried bitterly
on the lone pillow
for the gay Ukrainian skirt
and my mother's wilful
short-sighted love.

iv

I remember my own small ones
in a deluge of rain, Vancouver
being shepherded in their drooping costumes
on their first Halloween handout
and the shopping bags full of soggy
peanuts and apples—
never eaten

v

O yes I remember
Halloweens and Halloweens
(a quaint Canadian custom)
and the chance
                   once every year
to act out the fantasy
overturn garbage pails
                   in the witchwoman's garden
and to steal brass bells
(not meaning to steal them)
only wanting
to hear them   bell over bell
ringing   ringing
the wordless song

On Seeing

Far-fetched, the eye of childhood sees the whole
Essentializes figures to the brief
Recording of a rounded head
And outlets for the senses—
Eyes   ears   astonished hands;
And then takes on at puberty
A pained perception of the detailed self—
An agonizing analyst with eyes
Shaped to the comic strips
And women puffed like robins for a worm.

The inward eye begins as infantile
Sees only the broad outline of the self;
Until some blinding day
When stricken on Damascus way
The details are revealed:
Gnarled hands of age   distorted love
The skin of sickness stretched upon a soul;
The look "I hate"   the voice "I scorn"
The cry upon the deadly thorn:

This clarity is mercy for our sight:
Deformed, we seek the therapy of light.

Invisible Sun

Life is a pure flame, and we live by an invisible sun
within us
                                    –Sir Thomas Browne

At the end of a day my hands hold heat;
Dipped in the fire of love, they burn
Like radiant isotopes, to illustrate
Where hours went: hot in the washing water

Then seeking cellar shadows, cool cupboards
Where light of day shines from jewelled jellies:
Or upstairs in empty sleeping places
Tucking the light into a white sheet.

Oh, my hands have sung, have swung from the
        sun's centre
To be the veins of warmth within a room:
To burn with the work done and the night to
        come—
Rounded in sleep, to shape an invisible sun.

Grandmother

O lovely raw   red   wild
outward turned
it's time to think of the blood
and the red searing

pale   pale   the poets and poetasters
moving along the midnight mists
those riverbanks where girls
white flanked, never refuse
yield all their mysteries

Give me instead
a small child noting
holly and rowan berry ripen
a small hand clasped

Who is there? What's that?
O, to survive
what must we do
to believe?
In the trees, my grandson.
In these roots. In these leaves.

Ballad of the Battered Children

    We have made a deal
    have learned how to inhibit
    the spiked dark:
    we inhabit
    blue utopias
    wave
    radiant rags of cloud

We are summoned
to the death cell
after the hangman
in the brown checked suit
rosy cheeks
silver hair
has sat with us at the judgment table
His children sit there too
listening to the judge
who is our father
cawing out words from the text in the bible

The parents are in league
have judged us
to be the culprits
laying down our sins
for all to see
The parents have willed us
our death
the hangman rises, ready

    But we have made a deal
    with the powers of light!
    Before their accusing finger
    their cursing cries
    we vanish into
    our blue horizon.

On Reading Some Writings By Women

Sometimes I think of a swallow
beating its wings
against a wire mesh:
if she pulls her wings
tight   tight
will she get through?

Or I think of a child
hitting its fists against granite rock
when there're no doors
Mama she cries, *Mama*

Or a bee
blindly bumbling
against a window pane:
my helping hand
creates more confusion

The woman inside that box
called "home"
cannot wrench off
the roof

Always alone
These lost ones are
while their mates
are standing around
laughing

Life Styles

A city street
a corner
a nest
    is always
    over-peopled

but I accept
the situation
enjoy the tucked-in
kosher grocer
listen with silent laughter
to the sweet
private Hebrew lingo
demand
my buttermilk
my yogurt
FRESH!

I'm so lucky:
Can fly off
beside the rivering waters
cabined and closed
facing the sunset
that fans the fast-flowing
river   Opposite
are the shivering yellow woods
sturdy   enduring

I'd like to think
we will never give up
the two life-styles:
smell
of the teeming, jostling city
and life surrounded
by elms   oaks   maples

harbouring bluejays and squirrels:
scent of earth   fast flowing water
gold drift of leaves—

I'd like to think
my grandchildren
would understand—
breathe hard—
seize onto these
two ways of being human.

Parenthood

My child is like a stone
in wilderness
pick it up and rub it on the cheek
there's no response
or toss it down ...
only a hollow sound
but hold it in the hand
a little time
it warms   it curves
softly into the palm:
even a stone takes on a pulse
in a warm hold.

Friday's Child

I endowed you with the contents
of my anxious state
And it was not good

I willed you my brush and
        my fine-toothed comb
with their dusty hairs
And it was not pretty

In the afternoons of my discontent
I pulled up weeds in the back garden
And dressed you in them

When I walked at the seashore
moaning with the gulls
I pinned a black crow
on your shoulder

You have inherited all my pain
but only half my laughter
And it is not good

You are burdened, my little sister
And I cannot lift the stone
        from your heart

Where I Usually Sit

Where I usually sit
is by the south window
with the sun
pouring in   over me
and the magenta
cyclamen   with dark green
hearts   for leaves
beside me   on the table.

The school is opposite.
Where I usually sit
is full of children
              flying on ice
sliding from the grim green door
zut! into the street
or along the low rail fence
loaded with snow
turning somersaults   in winter.

Where I usually sit
there are rowans   clustered
              with red berries
frosted with snow
and a magpie   zooming
from branch to branch
the traffic churns
on deserts of uncleared roadway
turning the white
to smudge.

Here at this window
I toss words back and forth
on the typewriter
I yearn
for friends and loves   far off
warmed by the coastal waters

I sorrow   a little
that I'm only an aging person
onlooker
petrified   behind glass

And yet
from where I usually sit
my feet slide and skate
my arms   gesticulate ...
I stay in love with movement
hug   hug
the dancers
this world's youngest
most daring   dancers.

Rites of Passage

Rites of passage are generally recognized within the context of the adolescent's struggle towards individual identity. In my view, however, these stages of ritual passage also characterize the search for *relationship* between a man and woman – the phases of love.

Marriage, blessed or unblessed, is a pioneering job. There is no guide.

I

Song from The Multitude

Hushing the roar of towns
And their brief multitude.
            —Edward Thomas

They say the whip-poor-wills are singing in that wood:
I have not heard them.
They say that in the cool of evening-time
This June lies hushed to hear the throbbing note
So clear, so golden, of the hermit-thrush.
They say "The apple-bloom has fallen: Mickey has kittens—
Four, fluffy and black; Anna and I
Drove into town on Saturday night in the cart—
Such a blaze of lights! We had forgotten it all:
Winter makes such a difference, closes you in."
They say all this, these quiet trivial things:
But there, behind the words, clearly as now
I see the factory chimney-stacks, I see
The red-brick farmhouse heavy under the lilacs
The gloom, the aching sweetness of June dusk
Guarded by elms and tapering lombardies
And out in the clover fields or the pasture lands
The long thin fingers of the sun stretch out,
Linger in search of quietness, and touch
Caressingly the grass and the purple vetch.

If I could draw a curtain over my mind
As I have drawn so many, many times
A curtain across this city window-pane,
O then I might blot out the memory
So sharp, so luminous, of field and wood,
And never know again the ache to touch
Even one blade of grass clean of the dust.
Then I could turn within, turn to my work

73

In the house and learn these other narrow ways
Where knowledge is enclosed in parallels,
Street upon street. Then I need not wait
In hunger for your step to come, your arms
To hold me and your voice to hush.

It is not wise for any woman thus to be
So helpless when alone, with no reserves
To fall upon save a blank kitchen wall,
The meaningless ticking of a kitchen clock.
This narrow life, these walls to beat against,
This little space of floor when my quick feet
Would fain run miles upon a country road
Stumbling and falling, yet flying, flying on:
This is too difficult, when yet I see
Crows pressing northward, marsh-hawks crying; and hear
The wary whispered wind scratching the door.
Simply to fight despair, I dance, I sing,
I whirl as if in joy from room to room
And try to show the chairs how gay I am!
But not until I force the table-legs
To caper through the hall, will my dull heart
Be light again, my laughter be like wind.
Not until the mad impossible day
Arrives, when you and I return again
To the wide heaven and the farstretched earth,
And know ourselves through knowing quietness.
Not until then, dear love, will there be joy
To cover us with gold, a sun-like web.

"It is enough," you say, "to be content
To walk out in the evenings under a sky
Far off and cool, and hear the high clear sounds
Of children calling, women singing, organ-grinders
Winding out the old interminable song.
It is enough to be content with love."
Sometimes in the dark, in the night
When the walls dwindle and the sky creeps down
When there seem only stars for a roof, to my eyes
Tight-closed, and you so safely beside me,

74

No more than yourself, with some strange breath of my own
To quicken the fire that is you, the flame that is I—
Then in the dark, in the night, I cry out, I say:
"This is enough! I need no comfort more."

But let day come: morning shut out from me
By blinded buildings and by chimney-stacks.
Then I am starved for sun, and need
His mantle to go wandering in
And need his golden hammer-strokes
To quicken my slow pulse.

Therefore I say in all the beggar prayers
You do not hear, love is a prisoned place,
Love is a darkness with one blinding lamp
To lighten it, where ever our tired eyes
Must gaze unswervingly, or else we lose
All sense, all sight. Therefore I cry alone,
Let me go, let me fly away, let me find peace
Untroubled by the warring of two selves,
Cool as the dim recesses of a wood.
After too much music who desires
Anything but silentness, any tune
But windy fragments sounded in the grass?
After too much singing, who would not
Forget all words, stand quite still and watch
The silent sun follow the silent stars,
The moon without a sound rise up and pass
All unprotesting through the voiceless sky?
So there is too much passion in this flower:
I am enchained, imprisoned by your words,
Your look, and even less than these—your coat,
Hung upon a nail, which every time
I pass I cannot keep from touching: so,
By little things you hold me from the door,
Bid me to sing within; when some far voice
Integrally my own, is hushed, is dumb.

Page One

Reared on snow she was
Manacled in ice
Ten frostbound winters of her life
In bondage to this Lear
This blue lipped, fondling father
Whose hard chains
Clanked on her feet
Pinched the poor fingers stiff with pain.
Play, an ordeal to be endured
As feathery snow
Festooned the faces
Ridiculed the shapes
A rigid fence
Lay bundled on the hill
And snow made ladies out of trees
Those bare and gangling boys.

Feasted on snow
And cold's glass palaces she knew
The ice yard where huge blocks were river flung
To fortress out a field
And in the corridors of crisp
And rainbow shafted crystal
She traced the pattern of a princess' day
And was her godmother
And listened to her pray.

O might there always be
Those wishes three
That dazzling evanescent dress
Those pearls, those tears
That slipper made of glass—

But not for me.

But not for me
Whistled the winter wisdom of the wind:
The ice that bound her could not be her home
Native this land, but not
The boundary of her home.

ii

When spring sneaked sucking at the snow
Its tongue devouring humps and hills
Sipping at icicles until they dripped
In ignominious patter on
The rude brown water barrel's yawn—
Then rivulets began to run
The sound of shovels rasped the air
Grinding on chunks embedded firm
Demanding still a further term;
And in the slush, all sparkle gone
Water began to make its home
To sigh and sing, to crack and swing
Its column in the underground.

At such a moment, such a day
Her head was lifted suddenly
Her ears believed, her heart heard
The sky's hallooing honking word.
Here, in this wasting winter, geese
Briefly for feeding came to rest
Here they were transients, who knew
Some other home lay farther on
Some grass upshaken
A forest to be taken;
And following their arrowed alphabet
Straining to see their jet-
Propulsion through the unstained sky
She felt her feet untried
Her winter thongs unpried.
She was a moving miracle of wing and sound
No one home hers, but all homes to be found.

Inheritance

In the rooms of my mind you pace
Sad parent, your own head thorned—
Not in my power to bestow or bless
No gesture for surcease.

Some silence there was: sun's fierce
Assertion on a windy height,
Some daylight peace. But none to pierce
Shouting abyss, and raving night.

They called you shy; a blusterer—
Two poles, stretched agony between
And some might wonder why the grass grew green
Where acid words had lately been.

In the rooms of my heart you race
Fiery father of us, your kind,
Your burdened brood; who yet will face
The day, the dark; housed in a quiet mind.

Easter

Painful the probing spring
pernicious for
those who refuse
growth, for fear.

And is there fear
in each incisive thrust
of white shoot from the dark
cold kingdom of the loam?
And in each awkward wing
weaned from a leafy home?

Or is the human young alone
the unaccepting one
afraid to face the sun
or green fires of the bone?

Wedlock

Flesh binds us, makes us one
And yet in each alone
I hear the battle of the bone:
A thousand ancestors have won.

And we, so joined in flesh
Are prisoned yet
As soul alone must thresh
In body's net;

And our two souls so left
Achieve no unity:
We are each one bereft
And weeping inwardly.

The Husband

My guardian angel is a forbidden man.
Banned from the garden, he forbids
all others entry.
He wears no sword, but turned it long ago
into a pilgrim's ploughshare:
Presbyterian, he paints the earth more black
the heaven more radiant white
than my plain eyes perceive.

My landscape's technicolour: paradise,
the plummetings and plumes from colour's prism;
I, colour's prisoner, am gardened by love's green
dance the eternal daylight on a shaft of sun.
What do you guard then?   Adam? Or Quixote?
My freedom lies within.
O arbitrary gates and perilous walls!
Your bounden duty staggers out of bounds.

Letter at Midnight

Behave to me with love:
I am one so self-encircled
Only a thoroughbred could hurdle
These tough hedges.

And there are traps beyond
Set by the cunning of hated hand

And crags to clamber
Only a bold surefooted beast
Would venture.

Behave to me with love:
I am a country field, untamed
Restless for rider.

The Morning After

I cannot weep again, although the tears
Came easily before—
Life on the fringe of feeling—
Now hard sense builds me a solid door
Where I survey the morning.

Red poppies were uprooted in the night
Dishevelled silken bloom
Mud-spotted on the tiling
And every hope down-fallen in swift doom
And every dream divided.

But growing still goes on, persistence lives
In tug of a child's hand
In voicing his question—
Tears will not build again the house long planned
Nor man the bastion.

The Three Emilys*

These women crying in my head
Walk alone, uncomforted:
The Emilys, these three
Cry to be set free—
And others whom I will not name
Each different, each the same.

Yet they had liberty!
Their kingdom was the sky:
They batted clouds with easy hand,
Found a mountain for their stand;
From wandering lonely they could catch
The inner magic of a heath—
A lake their palette, any tree
Their brush could be.

And still they cry to me
As in reproach—
I, born to hear their inner storm
Of separate man in woman's form,
I yet possess another kingdom, barred
To them, these three, this Emily.
I move as mother in a frame,
My arteries
Flow the immemorial way
Towards the child, the man;
And only for brief span
Am I an Emily on mountain snows
And one of these.

And so the whole that I possess
Is still much less—
They move triumphant through my head:
I am the one
Uncomforted.

*Emily Brontë, Emily Dickinson, and Emily Carr.

Epithalamium for Susan*

i

A name beats in my blood—
Similkameen!
River of cool caress
and sudden flood
over whose veins we rode
gay and rough-shod.

That was a bridal ride
into Similkameen
with Indian as guide
and lover by my side
over the Skagit bluff
September scorched
where mountains opened up
mirror on mirror
each a reflection of
the other's face—
message of love
from a further place.
We moved from frame to frame
into a land unmapped
and crying for name;
our horses' hooves
beat a new alphabet
on mountainside and lake
calling out:
Skagit, Cedars, Cayuse Creek:
the trail was tried!

*Susan Allison, née Moir, who on her wedding night rode over the Hope-Princeton Trial to become "the first white woman of the Similkameen." Later the Allisons settled at Westbank on Lake Okanagan.

ii

At night the tales I heard
from Yacum-Tecum and I-cow-mas-ket
around our campfire, stirred
from centuries lost
from caves of silence drawn—
of satyr, shuswap and of giants born
invisible, save to the Indian eye—
those fiery myths breathed life into the stones
and made the boulders move
(I dared to touch one, and let loose a cry:
I was burned through.)

iii

So it was true, as you
long afterwards accused:
I did not give myself to you.
For on that wedding-night
I was a girl bound over to the hills,
my essence pierced with arrows of night air—
tang of sagebrush and the clear
perfume of pine.
No linen sheets for marriage-bed, but I
lay soft on "mountain feathers"—spruce,
mouth stained with huckleberry juice;
as epithalamium I heard
the deep drum's beat, the gutteral song
sounding in my blood and bone:
the river pounding loud and long
calling me home—Similkameen!

Latter Day Eve

But supposing (only supposing)
it was God himself, not Satan
who held up the forbidden fruit
above her vision
(and not an apple—the biblical "fruit"—
but a cluster of cherries?)
He   an old roué   lusting
held up over her head
the glowing cherries
and it was Adam
young   virile   eager
who plucked one   swiftly
and popped it into her mouth.
Ah, sweetness!
the sweetness of ripe cherry.

When they were ushered out
into a world of teeming traffic
demolition deluge
cranes screeching
scaffolds folding
yellow caterpillars churning up
the lost
the last dimension
she glued herself to a telephone pole
and panicked, hoarsely:
where are you
Adam?
Adam   where are you?

At the motel desk
she held up her room-key
so he would surely
see
but his eyes gazed steadily past her

at some disappearing waitress
and she flashed the key
fruitlessly!

Look to the End*

And if I hurt my knee
my good leg shows my poor leg
what to do

and if I hurt my arm
my good arm rubs my poor arm
into place

and if I hurt an eye
my good eye sees beyond the other's range
and pulls it onward   upward
into space

The sun's eye warms my heart
but if my good heart breaks
I have no twin
to make it beat again

Respice ad finem, the Livesay motto

Heritage

i

My father lived lusty but fearful
I am lusty and fearful

My father spoke his mind
sharply
I am sharp

He wrestled to lay the truth
and found her hard going
and sometimes he stumbled on stones
and turned by the wayside
and drank himself
maudlin

Sometimes I drink too—
too much
and sleep it off
in stony dreams

My father died
a sick, unhappy man—
let me die sooner!
not in bed, like him

      but walking   running
        leaping in the sun

ii

My father's crest
   is the lion's gamb
I wear his ring
   ask who I am

Aware so quickly
    of the burdened body
shrivelling eyes
    withered chin

Yet alive! to move with the dancer
    stamping within—
he sets me down softly
    on the lion's skin.

Other

i

Men prefer an island
with its beginning ended:
undertone of waves
trees overbended.

Men prefer a road
circling   shell-like
convex and fossiled
forever winding inward.

Men prefer a woman
limpid in sunlight
held as a shell
on a sheltering island ...

Men prefer an island.

ii

But I am mainland
O I range
from upper country to the inner core:

from sageland   brushland   marshland
to the sea's floor.

Show me an orchard where I have not slept
a hollow where I have not wrapped
the sage about me   and above   the still
stars clustering
over the ponderosa pine   the cactus hill.

Tell me a time
I have not loved,
a mountain left unclimbed:
a prairie field
where I have not furrowed my tongue,
nourished it out of the mind's dark places;
planted with tears unwept
and harvested as friend   as faces.

O find me a dead-end road
I have not trodden
a logging road that leads the heart away
into the secret evergreen of cedar roots
beyond sun's farthest ray—
then, in a clearing's sudden dazzle
there is no road; no end; no puzzle.

But do not show me! For I know
the country I caress:
a place where none shall trespass
none possess:
a mainland mastered
from its inaccess.

Men prefer an island.

Ballad of Me

i

Misbegotten
born clumsy
bursting feet first
then topsy turvy
falling downstairs;
the fear of
joy of
falling.

Butterfingers
father called it
throwing the ball
which catch as catch can
I couldn't.

Was it the eyes' fault
seeing the tennis net
in two places?
the ball flying, falling
space-time team-up?

What happened was:
the world, chuckling sideways
tossed me off
left me wildly
treading air
to catch up.

ii

Everyone expected guilt
even I—
the pain was this:
to feel nothing.

Guilt? for the abortionist
who added one more line
to his flat perspective
one more cloud of dust
to his bleary eye?

For the child's
'onlie begetter'
who wanted a daughter?
He'll make another.

For the child herself
the abortive dancer?

No. Not for her
no tears.
I held the moon in my belly
nine month's duration
then she burst forth
an outcry of poems.

iii

And what fantasies do you have?
asked the psychiatrist
when I was running away from my husband.
Fantasies? fantasies?
Why surely (I might have told him)
all this living
is just that
every day dazzled
gold coins falling
        through fingers.
So I emptied my purse for the doctor
See! nothing in it
but wishes.
He sent me back home
to wash dishes.

iv

Returning further now
to childhood's *Woodlot*
I go incognito
in sandals, slacks
old sweater
and my dyed
hair

I go disarrayed
my fantasies
twist in my arms
ruffle my hair

I go wary
fearing to scare
the crow

No one remembers Dorothy
was ever here.

II

Lament

for J.F.B.L.

What moved me, was the way your hand
Lay in my hand, not withering,
But warm, like a hand cooled in a stream
And purling still; or a bird caught in a snare
Wings folded stiff, eyes in a stare,
But still alive with the fear,
Heart hoarse with hope—
So your hand, your dead hand, my dear.

And the veins, still mounting as blue rivers,
Mounting towards the tentative finger-tips,
The delta where four seas come in—
Your fingers promontories into colourless air
Were rosy still—not chalk (like cliffs
You knew in boyhood, Isle of Wight):
But blushed with colour from the sun you sought
And muscular from garden toil;
Stained with the purple of an iris bloom,
Violas grown for a certain room;
Hands seeking faïence, filagree,
Chinese lacquer and ivory—
Brussels lace; and a walnut piece
Carved by a hand now phosphorus.

What moved me, was the way your hand
Held life, although the pulse was gone.
The hand that carpentered a children's chair,
Carved out a stair
Held leash upon a dog in strain
Gripped wheel, swung sail,
Flicked horse's rein
And then again

Moved kings and queens meticulous on a board,
Slashed out the cards, cut bread, and poured
A purring cup of tea;

The hand so neat and nimble
Could make a tennis partner tremble,
Write a resounding round
Of sonorous verbs and nouns—
Hand that would not strike a child, and yet
Could ring a bell and send a man to doom.

And now unmoving in this Spartan room
The hand still speaks:
After the brain was fogged
And the tight lips tighter shut,
After the shy appraising eyes
Relinquished fire for the sea's green gaze—
The hand still breathes, fastens its hold on life;
Demands the whole, establishes the strife.

What moved me, was the way your hand
Lay cool in mine, not withering;
As bird still breathes, and stream runs clear—
So your hand; your dead hand, my dear.

This Arrow

This arrow strikes me with the force of light
As if sped from the sun and aimed by him
To burn me to the quick;
And though I walk the ordinary way
And none can see the shaft bi-secting me,
I am not whole; and shall not be again.
I am not whole, as flesh is known to be
But move divided; here, on earthy feet
There, flashed with heaven's heat.
O do not find me, do not seek to know
What shaft upholds and arms me from you so.

Widow

No longer any man needs me
nor is the dark night of love
coupled

But the body is relentless, knows
its need
must satisfy itself without the seed
must shake in dreams, fly up the stairs
backwards.

In the open box in the attic
a head lies, set sideways.

This head from this body is severed.

After Grief

Death halves us:
every loss
divides
our narrowness
and we are less.

But more:
each losing's an encore
of clapping hands
dreaming us on;
the same scene played once more
willing us grander than
we were:
no dwarf *menines*
but kings and queens.

And still, some say
death raises up
gathers the soul strong-limbed
above the common tide
to catch a glimpse
(over world's wailing wall)
of an exultant countryside.

Disasters of the Sun

i

O you old
gold garnered
incredible sun
sink through my skin
into the barren bone

If I'm real
I'm totem carved
with your splayed
scalpel

If I'm a person
the gods roar
in horrible surprised
masculinity

but if I'm a woman
paint me
with the beast   stripes
assure me I am human

ii

The world is round
it is an arm
a round us
my fingers touching Africa
your hand
tilting Siberian trees
our thoughts
still as the tundra stones
awaiting footprints
bright between our bones
shines the invisible sun

Though I was certain
we recognized each other
I could not speak:
the flashing fire
between us
fanned no words

In the airport circle   where
the baggage tumbled
all my jumbled life
fumbled
to find the one sweet piece
the clothing stuffed and duffled
labelled mine

and over across the circle saw
your dark hair, piercing eyes
lean profile, pipe in mouth.

>   Incredibly, you move.
>   You seem to dance
>   and suddenly
>   you stand beside me, calm
>   without surprise:
>
>   I cannot tell
>   what country you are from
>   we recognize each other
>   and are dumb
>
>   your hand   your hand
>   tense on your pipe
>   your look   *a soft bomb*
>   *behind my eyes*

iv

My hands that used to be leaves
tender and sweet and soothing
have become roots
gnarled in soil

my hands
tender as green leaves
blowing on your skin
pulling you up
into joyous air
are knotted bones
whitening in the sun

v

During the last heat wave
a sunflower
that had stood up straight
outstaring the June
sun
wilted   collapsed
under a pitiless July
sky

now in burning August
I close out the city
trembling under heat
the green trees visibly
paling—

I close and curtain off myself
into four walls
breezed by a fan
but the fan
fumes!
and suddenly it
BREAKS OFF   from the wall

whirls   across the room
to rip my forefinger.

I tell you
we live in constant
danger
under the sun   bleeding
I tell you

                    vi

Keep out
keep out of the way of
this most killing
northern sun
grower   destroyer

Sun, you are no goodfather
but tyrannical king:
I have lived sixty years
under your fiery blades
all I want now
is to grope for those blunt
moon scissors

                    vii

When the black sun's
gone down
connect me underground
root tentacles
subterranean water

no more lovely man can be
than he with moon-wand
who witches water

III

The Origin of the Family

Where my parents canoed
on the Red River
on Sunday afternoons
before coitus
before I was conceived

the river flows on
seventy years after
without a trace
of his paddle's grace
or her low laughter

It's all in my head
their conversation
their efforts at
conciliation—
the nagging question:
are we in love
or not?

Because, at long last
September 1, 1908
they went to church, took the train
to Whytewold on the lake
to a borrowed honeymoon cottage
mice scuttling over their faces
and in the morning
as he cooked the eggs and bacon
he swearing like a trooper
("I'd never heard him swear before—
and I've never got used to it")

Was it because
he had decided she wasn't a virgin?
She never knew till twenty years later
why he resented her body and her ways
and how she had no chance
ever to prove to him
her essential innocence.

Now that I am here,
a life they joined in making
I bear their burdens:
her guilelessness, his guilt.
I am the wishbone's centre
made of their two-pronged
rivalries.
To be free I must push out
into a new world's proffering
I must go down and enter
that darker cave
with only my burnt hands
as offering.

The Inheritors

That was the last house I had to let go—
my grandmother's.
I did not own it
but it owned my youth.

When the movers came
and took away, at last,
the tall hall what-not
with mirror, carved walnut spires,
and secret drawers
where I had found a young man's *billet doux*
"an invitation to call," 1898,

when the movers calculated
how to break the mirrored elegance
into three pieces
"to get it through the door,"
I felt my head also
twisted from my neck
my torso shunted blindly
into the hostile street.

Ah, Cousin, lucky inheritor
who would receive our grandmother's furniture
back in the Eastern Townships
where it was first carved,
I did not envy you your belongings
for they fill only into that small house
out west on Polson Avenue
set in a shower of hollyhocks.
They belong to memory
who possesses all ... all ...

And as for me?
I have few possessions.

F.R.L.

Last seen at Vancouver station
pleased I had come to settle her down
on the green plush seat:
  I'm looking forward to this journey.

her eyes still cornflower bright
surveying the blurred landscape

And nothing ahead   at the end of the line
but being alone
with hyacinths in spring   hugging a shaky table
among piles of newspapers   and *first editions*
houses of cards toppling
to be sorted   sold   bargained about
and a family tree to be nattered over
after long bus trips into cricketing silence
visiting graveyards
deciphering the snow-dishevelled
hieroglyphs on tombstones

Nothing ahead,
but she had mastered the lock,
in her hooked and freckled fingers
held the key to ongoing.

Everywoman   Every Man

Nailed to two crosses, his and hers,
the mother's
the father's
How to resurrect
is the intense question
How to make of thine
mine?
Out of such desperate inharmonies
to become
one human domain?

The pain of it held me
thisway   thatway   turning
through fiery furnaces
eternally burning

If I have come out of it
shining
calm   clear as glass
it is because
you   each one   kissed me goodnight
without reprisals
sent me to sleep
on earth's pillow
that solace   that green grass

I was allowed to dream

Why We Are Here

Some of us are here
because we were visited
at dawn
were given a third
ear

Some of us especially
are women
open
ever receiving
into

Layton says
"The womb
is such a diminutive room
in which to lie"

But some of us are here
to say   *lie down*
children of men
lie down on the stiff brown stubble
at noon   the ice
melting to puddles
lie down at noon
on hard soil
singing with underground
water
lie down
and let our hands bear you as rivers
to the sea's room.

Some of us are here
as messages
because in the small womb
lies all the lightning.

Rachel   Rachel

I walked alone through wilderness
seeking a certain stone
climbed jutting rocks   and tore
my hands on briar bone

I moved alone through barriers
of thistle, cattle dung
and saw, undressed of its red bark
the green arbutus hung

and came upon a mound, new heaped
and coffin-sized, and spread
roughly, without a flower there
for living or for dead

but on the parents' grave
a headstone put
son at the top
and daughter at the foot

Then ran I on alone and swung
on a wild wishing-tree
free from all parents   daughter   son—
no games   no games
just me.

The Whole Sun

How marvellous
is the bend of the knife
slicing my desires down
to crumbs

How amazing
is the return of autumn
when I was born
in a Winnipeg snowstorm
and am now
re-born

How casual
is my kiss
on the cheek of a stranger
man or woman
acknowledging
the wish-changer

To be complete
we must hold the whole sun
wholly
in the marrow of the bone

We must celebrate
how to be one
with everyone
yet forever alone

The Merger

When I was *two* people
I sought to rival the other
ego
to chasten it
subdue
always there was
an intermittent war

Now I am *one*
I go hand in hand
with myself
linking our laughters

The Unquiet Bed: Fire and Frost

Written on my return from Africa, these poems were fired by an intense love affair with a younger man. Behind the passion there is a growing sense of the polarities that exist between a man's nature and a woman's.

Culture versus nature is what an earlier poem, "Bartok and the Geranium," is all about. Poems may or may not follow classical patterns—they explode out of every day experience.

I

At Dawn

The going
and the coming of our love
holds me
in bed   unable
to move over from
your folded bones

Awake   I hear
the ferment
of your dreams
churning my pillow
as your arm swings
presses its light lever
gently upon my heart—

You turn
returning

and over all
my body's fingertips
day breaks
a thousand crystals

The Unquiet Bed

The woman I am
is not what you see
I'm not just bones
and crockery

the woman I am
knew love and hate
hating the chains
that parents make

longing that love
might set men free
yet hold them fast
in loyalty

the woman I am
is not what you see
move over love
make room for me

Four Songs

i

People will say
        I did it for delight
        you—for compassion

But long before
our bodies met
the bargain was
established, set

Give me the will, you said
and in return
and take from my fill
of passion

        You did it from design
        I—from compulsion

ii

It is the fire you love
not me   not both
burning my body
it envelops you
attracts the moth
and the murderer too

        Dido knew
        this fire
        and chose
        that funeral

iii

And yet you knew
            my hunger

            the body blunt
            needing the knife
            the forked light-
            ning of tongues

            your blow
            eased me so
            I lay   quiet
            longer

But thirst remains
            thirst for cool
            cool water
            the gesture of your hands'
            white fountains

iv

I drink now
no fiery stuff
burning the mouth
I drink the liquid flow
of words   and taste
song in the mouth

The Cave

i

I am the quivering needle to your north
the trembling arrow sped—
I never believed it
never thought me bound
until one night all night I lay
under your will and mind
and heard you play my secrets
over and over in your hand.

ii

Taking my body so
on the unquiet bed
you pretend no care
save the act done, said

pretend you do not come
save for self-seeking ease—
take me or leave me there
just as you please

only when you sleep
coiled within that cave
your dream awakes me and your voice:
O love, we hold, we have.

The Taming

Be woman. You did say me, be
woman.   I did not know
the measure of the words

        until a black man
        as I prepared him chicken
        made me listen:
        —No, dammit.
        Not so much salt.
        Do what I say, woman:
        just that
        and nothing more.

Be woman. I did not know
the measure of the words
until that night
when you denied me darkness,
even the right
to turn in my own light.

Do as I say, I heard you faintly
over me fainting:
be woman.

The Woman

Don't hurry, I might say
when you first enter in
but then the urge takes hold
and it is I who cry
O hasten, quick untie
the fearful knot of pain
O hurry hurry on
and down
break me again
(until the bliss begins)

When you make me come
it is the breaking of a shell
a shattering birth

how many thousand children
we have conceived!

The Touching

i

Caress me
shelter me now
          from the shiver
of dawn
'the coldest hour'

pierce me again
          gently
so the penis completing
          me
rests in the opening
          throbs
and its steady pulse
          down there
is my second heart
          beating

ii

Light nips the darkness
          a white frost
breaking in ripples
          on a dark ground
like light your kisses hover
          touching my nipples
under the cover

iii

Each time you come
          to touch   caress
me

I'm born again
                    deaf   dumb
each time
        I whirl
                part of some mystery
I did not make or earn
that seizes me
                each time
I drown
        in your identity
I am not I
        but root
                shell
                    fire
each time you come
I tear through the womb's room
        give birth
and yet   alone
        deep in the dark
        earth
I am the one   wrestling
the element re-born

Sorcery

My breasts are withered gourds
my skin all over   stiffens
shrinks—the pubic hair
bristles to an itch

Not to be touched and swept
by your arm's force
gives me the ague
turns me into witch

O engineer of spring!
magic   magic me
out of insanity
from scarecrow into girl again
then dance me   toss me
catch!

The Notations of Love

i

You left me nothing, when
you bared me to the light
gently took off all my skin
undressed me to the bone

you left me nothing, yet
softly I melted down
into the earthy green
grass grew between my thighs

and when a flower shot
out of my unclenched teeth
you left me nothing but
a tongue to say it with.

ii

in my mouth
no love ?
only cruelty   you say

take love   take love
is my reply
the hard way

twisted and sparse
to find   facing the rock
the fountain's force.

iii

Crow's feet your finger follows
circling my eyes

and on the forehead's field
a skeleton of leaves

Only the lips stay fresh
only the tongue
unsheathes its secret skin
and bolts
the lightning in.

iv

I used to think
that Siamese twins
occurred only
in Siam
once disabused
I find their trace
no matter where
I am

especially around
these absences
our minds are twins
they circle and unite
my left arm is your right arm
bound   even in flight

v

My legs stretched two ways   disparate
until you came
and joined them
(lying down between)
now, even when we separate
my legs coil close
and feet unite:
they form a pedestal
whereon I turn, in sleep
circling, serene—
no longer desperate.

vi

I was naked
and you clothed
me

so, in the dead
of night
you whisper-
ed
no other word
        of praise
you found, in day
bright light
to say

but day or night, I
am undressed

dance
differently.

Moving Out

Dismantling our house
the features of our love are gone
our feet grow loud
in a bare room
arms long to lean
in softness between sheets
but all the paraphernalia and props
are out of reach

I can only stretch
for your arms now
and find an upright bed
between you bones—
without the body of your house
I'd have no home.

II

The Male Muse

Thank god I waited till you came!
How many false purveyors of the truth
of poetry
knocked at my door
declared the holy name

But you said nothing:
acted, only
demanded entrance
at the side door
of love

Now
sonnets brush through the cracks of the floor
music fans our fire

Let Your Hand Play First

Let your hand play first
fanning small fires
over the arms, the breasts
catching responses all along the spine
until the whole body flowering
's enveloped in one flame
that shudders wildly out
to meet your thrust—

Then burn, my fire
burn with a flame so tall
it can unshape the shaping clouds
unearthly move the sphere

Aubade

Not what you are
but what you are to me:
a stranger who's at home
inside my eyes
shoots rainbows
down my spine
laughs at my absurd
long second toe
and wags the world away
upon my tongue.
You are the one
who when I leap to leave you
for the sun
can pull me back to bed:
'Woman, Woman, *come.*'

Mistakenly

Mistakenly
your flowing into me
I took to be
yourself

When waters join
to form a river
neither claims
identity

Your hand becomes
familiar as my own
your heart-beats pulse
at my wrist-bone

And in your breathing
quietly
I feel your rhythm
timing me

The Search for Wholes

i

This is a good bed
It has two sides
a pull-out—for you
a permanent—for me

ii

If we are two halves
of the same fruit
why must we fight
over the stone?

iii

You say it is anticipation
whets your tongue
but I learned young
never to hope:
It's the unexpected
realization
catches my breath
sears my bone

Only Before Dawn

Only before dawn
is the world soundless
streets uncluttered
by footsteps or sirens
my heart unpounding
your body folded
sleeping
only before dawn
do I lie in a clear pool
almost unbreathing

But dawn is the coldest hour
and as it strikes, the furnace
downstairs   begins to roar!

You rouse, out of sleep
and seize me

In My Dream Room

In my dream room
you go and come

I have a window looking out
on sky
you linger there
and say
no clouds today

In my dream room
your meteorology
defies the storm
immobilizes
windy weather

This page my book

My life is on the right
track!   I cry
to the margins pushing me over and over
squeezing me out—
In the margins are all the notations
scribbled
sniffs of sun, sand
ribs of your bony structure
strands of your colourless hair
these beckon curl and wind
words to the edge of the page
fly out all over
               spill
                    from enchanted mouths
words, your words
        appear on the magic slate
my body rubs them out
        and I try again
             to defend the right hand
                      side
of the paper
        to leave myself room for breathing

Try to compete with wind?
          How?
Your avalanche of talk
          rains
            stains me over again
and the margins are taken over
invaded
by this sweet
            hot sweat
the notations of love

The Hard Core of Love

The hard core of love
is only muscle, thrust
to an intensity
of lust

I seek bones
pressed into me
rooted as stones
around my tree

I seek more
than skin, flesh, blood
I seek the coursing
heaving heart
for my soul's food

The Record of All Our Nights

The record of all our nights
is on these sheets:
though washed, held up in sunlight
the mark remains

So follow all the ads
Try out all the soaps
no bleach can take from linen
what the body wrote

When I Got Home

When I got home
there was a boot on my table—
under the chair
I found a sock suspended—
flung on the floor
      a man's jacket—
trousers leaped
      from the china cupboard

When I got home
I had no private ground:
the clothes whirred together
and you were in them
whirling me round

You Are My Mirror

You are my mirror   I
glance at all your side-
long selves
performing in the room
a baker's dozen
of characters

and I see me   the un-
seen partner   pirouetting
there   mocking your every
gesture with my own
babble and talk
mirror bubbles blown
up into unknown lanes
criss   crossing
the universe

> It's true   I've lied
> but you've lied too
> and laid down truth
> untenderly
>
> *You are the only one*
> *I never lie to*
>
> Go to   lay me   slap me
> with your bared
> truth

But conversation is   no
joy ride
never smooth
it hiccups   to
a stop

we wait
counting the heart
beats
afraid to see
in the rear-view mirror
eye
to eye
        In mirrors
        no one can touch

The Uninvited

Always a third one's there
where any two are walking out
along a river-bank   so mirror-still
sheathed in sheets
of sky   pillows of cloud—
their footprints crunch the hardening earth
their eyes delight in trees   stripped clean
winter-prepared
with only the rose-hips red
and the plump fingers of sumach

And always between the two
(scuffling the leave, laughing
and fingers locked)
goes a third lover   his or hirs
who walked this way with one or other   once
flung back the head   snapped branches of dark pine
in armfuls   before snowfall

        I walk beside you
        trace
        a shadow's shade
        skating on silver
        hear
        another voice
        singing under ice

Because We Want Each Other

Because we want each other
we think to take another
thus splitting all the atoms in the world
and all the mirrors, shattering

Because we want each other
we have scooped up time
a fistful in the hand
and galloped over space
Only, I cry to touch you where you stand
Only, you whisper, to stroke your gentle face

But since we can't go back
nor I be twenty-two again, with you
put me on ice, and then
at century's end
set me on fire!

I Touched

I touched
with insight's eye
across a street
the other woman whom you loved,

You are quite right:
how beautiful she is!
grave, sharply cut
strangely Egyptian

But in her eyebrow's arch
I see resemblances:
she has imprinted well
cruelty's mark

I Sought To Cut You From Me

I sought to cut you from me—
as well I'd tear
the stamen from a flower
and have it bear

as well I'd blind
the flying horses of the plain
and have them leap the sagebrush crevices
entangled in a chain

I sought with scalpel, cunningly
to amputate where love had set its seal:
you hold to life in darkness—
bright wound that will not heal

The Quarrel

It does not come from harm or hate

but from the rages and the guilt

that love necessitates

It does not come from being bound

to love the other,   but

from being free

It does not use the silences

as cover

it wrests from speech

the necessary knife

And when the silence comes

(the peace beside the lover)

it renders up to sleep

the pain left over

Twice, Twice I Let You Go

Twice, twice I let you go
but love has fooled me
               fooled me
For you returned each time
more longing than the last
and sealed my eyes
and fevered my lids down
with burning sentences
melted my body into wax
and closed my mind.

Now eyes are sealed indeed and hot with salt
of my own tears
knowing the loss
feeling the emptiness
the walls of self are echoing
without your voice
the fire of laughter fading into air
without that passionate response—

O dear my dear
too long did I rehearse your going on
and now it's happened
I am chill, I mourn—
I hold a wood dove in my hand
his pulse with mine makes moan

Now It Is Done

Now it is done
and there is no
recrimination
the motives you suspect
I had, were all
in your imagination

And I saw who saw you
as magician, prince
frequenter of despair
now with massaging hand
I rub your spine—hard, tense—
ruffle your hair

There is between us now
no muddied water
and above
no clouded sky
mocking our laughter

There is between us
only this
astonishing surprise
secret and sealed:
one body and one bliss
together healed

The Severance, Being Willed

The severance, being willed
not forced upon us
takes on dimensions other than
love hate; joy pain
profit and loss

And what we will remember is:
no evil crossed our lips
the toads' and vipers' hiss
vanished from our tongues
the sentences we found
created their own structures
out of bliss

The Operation

And I too
after the blaze of being   alive
face the wall
over which breath must be thrown

faced the wall
scratched by graffiti   of trying
and made there
my trembling mark

Where the knife was poised
a warm flame leaped   between us
I   victim
grateful to be saved
and he   appraising
how to create from bone and flesh
a new woman?
the needle shot into my arm
and I was his

In the dazed days that followed
he used to appear
in silent white precision
at my door
and stand there till I recognized
him   surgeon—
a nod: he waited with pursed lips
eyes quizzical beneath the furry brows
until I raged and ranted—
or docile on blue mornings
acknowledged all
solicitudes—
between us still
that intimate   flashing bond

Now it is over! He pronounces health
I walk   near steady
out of his office   down his corridor
(the elevator sighs
the breath I fought for)
outside   pale
the autumn smog   the foul
snarl of commuting cars
the pavement's glare:
I have to breathe deep   here
to be alive again

ii

You pulled me back
into life
your very penis   forging
pulling
me   back
refrain   refrain
love me again
and when once
was all I gasped for
(still in pain)
you demanded more:
love me again

The second time I turned
swam with you into darkness
was the foetus
fed by blood
and breath
fighting to grow
gasping for air
world's door
—then drowned
and slept.

It is enough
I dreamed

but you
were ever again   there
over me   lord
over me cutting me open again
till the would cried
and you took my pain into your side
and lay there   healing me
with gentle breath and tongue
lulling me down
tender   rocking   ease
and a quick come.

                    iii

Later   the seasons came
and changed
this loving was a sickness   too
in which we said farewell
so many times
and each goodbye a prelude   prescope
            of the next
swung needles deeper into flesh
            split the mind's peace
Listen!   when rain rattles the branches
            our ghost shivers

(a kind of disease between us
            love was
indulged in as excuse
            for going to bed
we transmitted kisses
and I caught between my thighs
            the antibody)

From my convalescent window
I see you cured
jay-walking on robson street
            a well man
                    free of opposites

it's cloudy still
rain
smirches the pane

Morning: I face
wet pavement   distorted
mirrors
              (green Christmas and your lean body
              lounging along the shore
              your lunging arms
              flung against boulders)

I decide to complete the operation
tear myself into four quarters
scatter the pieces
north
a crystal city of ice
arching up   stretching out daily
dazedly
into uncoiling
animal sun—
another kingdom

                    iv

Until I'd found a doorway
I could stand in   push against
I did not know how shrunk
I had become
for the *he*   the *you*   are one
and gone
and I must measure me

O let me grow
and push
upright!
ever aware of height
and the cry
to reach a dazzled strangeness
sun-pierced sky

The Step Beyond

The doorway appeared
    luminous
as if light were music
    and music light
The doorway
     appeared
           (a door is for seeking
               the hand outstretched
             to touch)

But on reaching
    forces beyond
      pushed backwards
I fell into old patterns
took up my sewing
    in a confined room

but ever so often
    hearing a bird's cry
      (that evening thrush, fluting)
sparrows twittering their delight in daylight

saw walls give way
and the doorway looming
    luminous
      there

Eventually
was able to stand
      unswaying
and blink away world's blackness
to discern the vision: blue green
essence of bird flashing
his colours weaving   a wild song

Struggle: The Documentaries

As Canada emerged from the "Dirty Thirties," Canadian radio was also emerging as a powerful force. I had been quite excited by the American documentaries by Archibald MacLeish, written for radio and stage, and also by the documentary film experiments of John Grierson. Both MacLeish and Grierson returned more and more often to the need for the artist to speak with a public voice. I identified myself with a whole world movement of poets writing politically-oriented social criticism and was fired with the desire to set down what was happening to my Canadian generation, historically and socially.

Although definitely written with radio in mind, my poems about the Depression, such as "Day and Night" and "West Coast: 1943" were not aired on the CBC. However, my turn came with the documentary about the Japanese-Canadians, "Call My People Home," produced on CBC in 1949 and again in 1952. Three post-war documentaries, "Zambia," "Prophet of the New World," and "The Raw Edges (1981)," were published but not produced. This has been a source of regret for me because I think, as I have written recently, a poem is an archive for our times.

In defense of the poet as unacknowledged legislator, I like to quote an English poet of the thirties, C. Day Lewis:

> "We make art of the quarrel with others, rhetoric," Yeats has said, "but of the quarrel with ourselves, poetry"....This conception...expresses the opposition between the divided selves of the poet; his poetic self and his human self, a conflict of which Yeats has always been acutely aware. Yeats's own magnificent political poems...are sufficient proof that a deep feeling about political ideas and events is not necessarily synonymous with that "quarrel with others" which produces only rhetoric.*

Deliberately then, I have chosen to reprint some poems that sprang out of these ironies and dichotomies; and some where hope flies free.

*C. Day Lewis, *A Hope for Poetry*, 1936.

Day and Night

i

Dawn, red and angry, whistles loud and sends
A geysered shaft of steam searching the air.
Scream after scream announces that the churn
Of life must move, the giant arm command.
Men in a stream, a moving human belt
Move into sockets, every one a bolt.
The fun begins, a humming, whirring drum—
Men do a dance in time to the machines.

ii

One step forward
Two steps back
Shove the lever,
Push it back

While Arnot whirls
A roundabout
And Geoghan shuffles
Bolts about.

One step forward
Hear it crack
Smashing rhythm—
Two steps back

Your heart-beat pounds
Against your throat
The roaring voices
Drown your shout

Across the way
A writhing whack

Sets you spinning
Two steps back—

One step forward
Two steps back.

iii

Day and night are rising and falling
Night and day shift gears and slip rattling
Down the runway, shot into storerooms
Where only arms and a note-book remember
The record of evil, the sum of commitments.
We move as through sleep's revolving memories
Piling up hatred, stealing the remnants,
Doors forever folding before us—
And where is the recompense, on what agenda
Will you set love down? Who knows of peace?

Day and night
Night and day
Light rips into ribbons
What we say.

I called to love
Deep in dream:
Be with me in the daylight
As in gloom.

Be with me in the pounding
In the knives against my back
Set your voice resounding
Above the steel's whip crack.

High and sweet
Sweet and high
Hold, hold up the sunlight
In the sky!

Day and night
Night and day
Tear up all the silence
Find the words I could not say...

iv

We were stoking coal in the furnaces; red hot
They gleamed, burning our skins away, his and mine.
We were working together, night and day, and knew
Each other's stroke; and without words, exchanged
An understanding about kids at home,
The landlord's jaw, wage-cuts and overtime.
We were like buddies, see? Until they said
That nigger is too smart the way he smiles
And sauces back the foreman; he might say
Too much one day, to others changing shifts.
Therefore they cut him down, who flowered at night
And raised me up, day hanging over night—
So furnaces could still consume our withered skin.

Shadrach, Meshach and Abednego
Turn in the furnace, whirling slow.
    Lord, I'm burnin' in the fire
    Lord, I'm steppin' on the coals
    Lord, I'm blacker than my brother
    Blow your breath down here.

    Boss, I'm smothered in the darkness
    Boss, I'm shrivellin' in the flames
    Boss, I'm blacker than my brother
    Blow your breath down here.
Shadrach, Meshach and Abednego
Burn in the furnace, whirling slow.

v

Up in the roller room, men swing steel
Swing it, zoom; and cut it, crash.

Up in the dark the welder's torch
Makes sparks fly like lightning reel.

Now I remember storm on a field
The trees bow tense before the blow
Even the jittering sparrows' talk
Ripples into the still tree shield.

We are in storm that has no cease
No lull before, no after time
When green with rain the grasses grow
And air is sweet with fresh increase.

We bear the burden home to bed
The furnace glows within our hearts:
Our bodies hammered through the night
Are welded into bitter bread.

Bitter, yes:
But listen, friend:
We are mightier
In the end.

We have ears
Alert to seize
A weakness
In the foreman's ease

We have eyes
To look across
The bosses' profit
At our loss.

Are you waiting?
Wait with us
After evening
There's a hush—

Use it not
For love's slow count:

Add up hate
And let it mount

Until the lifeline
Of your hand
Is calloused with
A fiery brand!

Add up hunger,
Labour's ache
These are figures
That will make

The page grow crazy
Wheels go still,
Silence sprawling
On the till—

Add your hunger,
Brawn and bones,
Take your earnings:
Bread, not stones!

vi

Into thy maw I commend my body
But the soul shines without
A child's hands as a leaf are tender
And draw the poison out.

Green of new leaf shall deck my spirit
Laughter's roots will spread:
Though I am overalled and silent
Boss, I'm far from dead!

One step forward
Two steps back
Will soon be over:
Hear it crack!

The wheels may whirr
A roundabout
And neighbour's shuffle
Drown your shout

The wheel must limp
Till it hangs still
And crumpled men
Pour down the hill

Day and night
Night and day
Till life is turned
The other way!

West Coast: 1943

This hour: and we have seen a shabby town change face,
the sandy soil be stripped of evergreen
and broom, born yellow into golden May
scrapped farther up Grouse Mountain. We, who lay
in roses and green shade under the cherry tree
we too were rooted up, set loose to beg
or borrow a new roof, accept a poorer view.
The tide had turned. That early gull adrift
on empty inlet, keel to sun, he was outrun
by humming plane, the flying boat on trial;
and pleasure schooner skirting the dark shore
was soon forced into harbour; for the grey gaunt giants,
hunters of skyline, convoy cruisers, they
jostled the bay.
              We saw the shoreline ripped
and boxes set in tidy rows, a habitation for
a thousand children swept from farm and mine
drawn to the hungry suction of the sea;
and saw the sunny slip where ferries sauntered in
easing their stragglers into a sleepy street
suddenly ablaze! And walls reared up, ship high,
grim curtain for machine-gun rat-tat-tat
as caulkers set to work and welders steered
the starry shrapnel on a new-laid keel.
Where two or three had come, travellers to be met
or mountain hikers holidaying high,
now in a herd of thundering hard heels
men surged for shop and ways, ten thousand strong
and bent for business, eager to belong.

High on our hill we watched, and knew
morning become high noon, and the tide full.
He who knew heaven is coming down the mountain
is stirred with wonder; curious, even he,

who bent eyes bookward in his earliest days
sucking the sunlight from a world of words
dreaming to be word-welder, builder of these.
Then up, and thoughts away, and books stamped under
up to the gravelled trail, the crags far yonder
where sun and rain blazed bliss on him
night chasing day on snow-spilt mountain rim.
He who knew heaven stands among us, watching
his hand unfitted to this hammer-hold,
his heart not conscious of the anvil-beat,
no visor for his eyes. Now he
makes ships? For carrying love in hold,
for salting down old wisdom into kegs
for other hands to welcome—yes and yes!
But ships for men to fight upon,
ships to right the wrong upon?—
He hardly knows; he hesitates.

And all about men flatten out the steel
with hammer beat, beat hammer, hammer beat,
shape it with sweat and muscle, shaped to fit
the muzzle of a ship, a new sea-bird.
And all about the masked men strike the torch
shaping the sides of ships with plate on plate
riveting bolts with sea-resistant spark.
From ship to ship, galley to hold, the pattern-makers move
until a new keel's laid, another scaffolding;
till fire and sweat, muscle and oath and jest
mingle to launch her down the vaulted ways—
a pearl-grey pointer leashed against the quays.

And why? What heaven-sent wanderer
could see the anthill swarm, and be at ease?
Could carry a load of tools or wheel a truck
to sling steel rods onto a derrick train?
He watched a day or so; waited his time
stood in the blacksmith's doorway where the furnaces
bellied and glared, vomiting molten steel
till the great moulder caught and shouldered it,
machine's male hands on feminine soft flesh

creating features, fittings for a bride—
a child of ocean still at berth, unscarred.

Challenged, mind moved, but not to the blood warmed
excitement seething in nerves' crevices
the ship, he saw, a symbol of conception
a giant scheme rearing to sky fruition.
But yet he stood without; a stranger still,
one hesitant to knock.

SHIPYARD VOICES

On morning shift, when sky and water melt
when men and women pour, with swinging pails
from ferry slip
pass through the gates, are billeted
and move, alert, toward the long grey shape
to find their home, their roof—
on morning shift, song burst from below the decks.
True as a bell, along the dock rang
Andalusian love song; high amidships
rumble of the rumba; in the hold
a youngster jived; and girls at hand
trousered and kerchiefed, busy hammering,
whistled clear the call to Coolins.
Song! Song from the throat of morning bursting
high above rivet, chipper, torch—
song from the hearts of men at labour
welding their words into the ship's side.

i

Who have from mountain wall
tunnelled to dark pits
where gas reeks, where weak light is life;
who have on mountain side,
meagre as table bare, taken a wife
made children, reared a roof;
who fought in strikes and met starvation
then back to pits again to face damnation

163

the dust sticking in throat, the cough, collapse.
Then from the Sanitarium, down to sea
to sea-coast air where men were building ships—
who breathe now, who find voice
and sing with the throat bare.

ii

Who have through hail and storm, through endless rain
cherished the crop, husbanded our flock.
Have builded fences, reared high dykes
shifted the barn to upper ground
and with the hay half harvested, seen cloud
crouch low again to pelt destruction down:
seen trees and fences, horses, calves and lambs
float helpless by, moaning their last faint cry—
who from despair and loss returned to city's arms
and at the sea gate found a silver ship.

iii

Who have loved water, yearned for flood
watched woolly clouds puffed from the piping sky
have held the crumbing firmament in hand
and knew no seeds could breathe, no green life flow;
who on the burnt spring grass cherished a crocus bloom
until we cursed it, for it bore no bread.
Who had no walls, no home
no animals in barn
only the rusted implements
only the thistle, self-sown.
Who trekked bare-footed, underfed
greedy for fruit in Okanagan fields,
thirsty for ocean even if salt it be:
who have paused here, on brink of life again
to build the ships and bless the autumn rain.

iv

Who have been reared on rations and soup-kitchens
and sent from school unlearned, clutching at work
riding the rods with hobos, drug fiends, college students
and sleeping, at the country's end, in flophouse—

Who have lain low, known thin girls in alley
kissed under a bridge and pillowed on stone
who raised a fist to window, blind with anger
and demonstrated hate in the streets of the sleek;
Who have been thrown a bone and yapped at thrower
who looked this gift horse sharply in the mouth
who work, watching; who launch ships, wary
waiting the year's turn, living to see...
We too are here, bent over bench and caulker
our hearts awake; for now, our voices free.

> He who knew heaven saw the gateway open
> heard the morning singing in the hold.
> He who knew heaven seized a rivet, hammer
> ran to new keel laid on ways, to new life set
> ready for use, ready to break or build.

FINALE

High on our hill we watched, and saw
morning become high noon, and the tide full.
Saw children chequered on the western beach
and ferry boats plough back and forth, knocking the nose
of tugboats, barges, freighters, convoys, cruisers:
the harbour a great world of moving men
geared to their own salvation, taking heart.
We watched gold sun wheel past the sombre park
slip beyond Lion's Gate, illuminate
cool purple skyline of the Island hills.
Then to the hulls and houses silence came
blinds down on tired eyes
dark drew its blanket over trees and streets
grey granaries and harbour lights; muffled the mountain-side.

165

Yet still, far, far below those lights pierced sky
and water; blue and violet, quick magenta flash
from welder's torch; and still the foreshore roared
strumming the sea, drumming its rhythm hard
beating out strong against the ocean's song:
the graveyard shift still hammering its way
towards an unknown world, straddling new day.

Montreal, 1933: Mass Chant

Dufferin Square is a playground
It's a dirty grey place downtown
But there are swings and seesaws:
Dufferin Square is a playground for children.
Hardly anyone plays there.
Along the benches, sitting near the sand-piles
Men with unchildlike, wrinkled faces
Are huddled together. In small groups
They dominate the playground
Solidly round the square they watch the wind,
Swinging the empty swings—
The seesaws point mutely upward.

We must remember: Archbishop Gauthier has spoken:
"Let us be glad that no one has died of starvation
In this country." We must remember
A few blocks away the tailor is making a suit
For Cuba's Machado. —He's not left his seclusion.
Soft carpets tell no tales and the hangings
Of deep velvet bear no bloody stains.

In Cuba the masses have not blundered!
In Cuba the masses know their foe!
In Dufferin Square the men talk in low voices,
In Dufferin Square the clenched fist fears the light.

Why? Why? Why?
Was Nick Zynchuk then murdered for nothing?

Have we no answer for the brutal arm?
Because we live in a city within a city—
At war with itself and its factions
This does not deny the fact of these skyscrapers
Made by the workers—these granaries
Filled with our wheat; these railways shining
Unloading to ships pointed out to the sea.
This does not deny the steel mills and textiles
That we are creating and building
Not separately—Polish, Italian and French
But with all our great strength together we're building.

Dufferin Square is a playground
Where big words sound lovely
But there are words being spoken
That hold meaning and action.
There are words beginning!
There are thoughts being lighted!
Cuba's Machado still fears the street.

Call My People Home

A Documentary Poem for Radio

ANNOUNCER:

Now after thirty years come from a far island
Of snow and cherry blossoms, holy mountains,
To make a home near water, near
The blue Pacific; newcomers and strangers
Circled again and shaped by snow-white mountains,
These put down their roots, the Isseis:*
The older generation. This is their story.

CHORUS OF ISSEIS:

Home, they say, is where the heart is:
Transplanted walls, and copper-coloured gardens
Or where the cherry bough can blow
Against your pain, and blow it cool again—
This they call home.

But for ourselves we learned
How home was not
Even the small plot, raspberry laden
Nor shack on stilts, stooping over the water,
Nor the brown Fraser's whirl,
Sucking the salmon upward.

Home was the uprooting:
The shiver of separation,
Despair for our children
Fear for our future.

*Isseis–generation born in Japan.

Home was the finding of a dry land
Bereft of water or rainfall
Where water is cherished
Where our tears made channels
And became irrigation.

Home was in watching:
The fruit growing and pushing
So painfully watered;
The timber hewn down
The mill run completed.

Home was in waiting:
For new roots holding
For young ones branching
For our yearning fading…

ANNOUNCER:

His ancestors had lived near water
Been fishermen under Fujiyama's shadow.
Each season in the new land found him struggling
Against the uncertain harvest of the sea,
The uncertain temper of white fishermen
Who hungered also, who had mouths to feed.
So these men cut his share
From half to one-eighth of the fishing fleet:
But still he fished, finding the sea his friend.

FIRST FISHERMAN:

Home was my boat: T.K. 2930—
Wintering on the Skeena with my nets
Cast up and down the river, to lure and haul
The dogfish. (His oil, they said, was needed overseas
For children torn from home, from a blitzed town.)
We made good money, and the sockeye run
That summer had outdone all the remembered seasons.
Now I could own my boat, *Tee Kay*, the Gillnetter
The snug and round one, warm as a woman

With her stove stoked at night and her lanterns lit
And anchor cast, brooding upon the water
Settled to sleep in the lap of the Skeena.

Now after thirty years, come from an island
To make a home near water: first on a sailing vessel
Towed, each season, to the fishing grounds:
Then the small gasboat, the gillnetter, that belonged
Not to the man who fished, but to the cannery.
Now after thirty years a free man, naturalized,
A man who owned his boat! I smelt the wind
Wetting my face, wave dashing against the *Tee Kay's*
    sides
The grey dawn opening like a book
At the horizon's rim. I was my own master—
Must prove it now, today! Stooping over the engine
Priming the starter, opening the gas valve,
I felt her throbbing in answer; I laughed
And grasped the fly wheel, swung her over.
She churned off up the river—my own boat, my home.

That was before Pearl Harbor: before a December day
Spent on a restless sea; then anchor in the dusk
And down to bunk to have a bowl of rice.
By lantern light I turned the battery set
To hear brief messages from fishermen
From boat to shore, to learn the weather forecast.
Must have been dozing when I woke up sharp—
What was he saying? Some kind of government order?
'All fishing craft on the high seas must head at once
To the nearest port, report to authorities.'
Did they not want our fish, the precious oil?
'No,' said the voice, 'Our boats were to be examined, searched
For hidden guns, for maps, for treachery...'
I heard, but could not understand. Obeyed,
But as a blind man. The numb fear about my boat,
Tee Kay, found no release in port, off shore,
Rubbing against a fleet of trollers, frail gillnetters
All heading down for Inverness and Tusk
All in the dark, with rumour flying fast.

No one knew more than his fear whispered,
No one explained.
We thought: perhaps it's all a mistake
Perhaps they'll line us up and do a search
Then leave us free for Skeena, Ucluelet—
The time is ripe, the season's fish are running.

SECOND FISHERMAN:

There was no mistake. It wasn't a joke:
At every fishing port more boats fell in.
Some had no wood, no gasoline; and some
Barely a day's store of food aboard.
So we waited at the Inlet's mouth, till the 16th.

FIRST FISHERMAN:

How speak about the long trip south, the last
We ever made, in the last of our boats?
The time my life turned over, love went under
Into the cold unruly sea. Those waves
Washing the cabin's walls
Lashed hate in me.

SECOND FISHERMAN:

We left Rupert in two long lines of sixty boats
Strung to the seiners, met and tugged
By *Starpoint* and the naval escort, the corvette.
All day we watched the gloomy sea roughed up
By westerlies, but had to tough it out
Glued to the wheel, weary for sleep, till 2 a.m.

Then, at Lowe Inlet, had brief anchorage.
At Milbanke Sound we ran into heavier seas
The buffeted boats like so many bobbing corks
Strung on a thin rope line that over and over
Would break, be mended by the corvette's men
And then again be snapped by snarling sea.

FIRST FISHERMAN:

Christmas at sea. The bitterest for me
That any year had given. Even so
Some had a celebration, pooled their funds
And bought the only chicken left in Alert Bay.
Others boiled cabbages in salt sea water,
Pulled out the playing cards and shrugged, and laughed.
As we set sail at midnight, now a thousand boats
Chained to the naval escort, steadily south
Into familiar waters where the forests cooled their feet
At rocks'-end, mountains swam in mist—
As we set sail for home, the young ones, born here, swore
Not softly, into the hissing night. The old men wept.

The rest takes little telling. On the fifteenth night
We passed Point Grey's low hulk, our long line wavered
    shoreward.
Dirty and hungry, sleep lying like a stone
Stuck in our heads, we nosed our broken craft
Into the wharf at Steveston, 'Little Tokyo.'
The crowd on the dock was silent. Women finding their men
Clung to them searchingly, saying never a word,
Leading them home to the *ofuro** and supper.
Others of us, like me, who knew no one,
Who had no place near the city's centre
Stood lonely on the wharf, holding the *Tee Kay's* line
For the last time, watching the naval men
Make a note of her number, take my name.
That was the end of my thirty years at the fishing
And the end of my boat, my home.

ANNOUNCER:

These their children, the Niseis,† were born
Into the new world, called British Columbia home,
Spoke of her as mother, and beheld
Their future in her pungent evergreen

ofuro–the bath.
†Niseis–generation born in Canada.

172

GIRL'S VOICE:

We lived unto ourselves
Thinking so to be free
Locked in the harbour
Of father and mother
The children incoming
The tide inflowing.
We lived unto ourselves
Locked in the harbour

BOY'S VOICE:

I remember the schoolhouse, its battered doorway
The helter-skelter of screaming children
Where the old ones went, my sisters
Soberly with books strapped over their shoulders:
Deliberately bent on learning—
(And learned, soon enough, of
The colour of their skin, and why
Their hair would never turn golden.)

GIRL'S VOICE:

But before the bell rang
For me
My turn at becoming
Before the bell rang
I was out on the hillside
Reaching high over my head for the black ones
The first plump berries of summer;
A scratch on the arm, maybe, a tumble
But filling my pail and singing my song
With the bees humming
And the sun burning.

Then no bell rang for me;
Only the siren.
Only the women crying and the men running.
Only the Mounties writing our names

173

In the big book; the stifled feeling
Of being caught, corralled.
Only the trucks and a scramble to find
A jacket, a ball, for the bundle.

My blackberries spilled
Smeared purple
Over the doorway.
Never again did I go
Blackberry picking on the hillside.
Never again did I know
That iron schoolbell ringing.

BOY'S AND GIRL'S VOICES:

The children incoming
The tide inflowing.

ANNOUNCER:

From the upper islands of the coast
With only one day's notice to depart
Came these, and hundreds like them: Mariko and her
    mother.
In the re-allocation centre, Hastings Park
Mariko writes a letter.

THE LETTER:

I wonder where in the inner country
On what train shooting between two mountains
You fly tonight, Susumu?
When I explain to you how it is here
You will understand, perhaps,
Why I have not been able to tell my mother
About you and me.

It is this: she is continually frightened—
Never having lived so, in a horse stall before.
My bunk is above hers, and all night I lie rigid

174

For fear to disturb her; but she is disturbed.
She has hung her pink petticoat from my bunk rail
Down over her head, to be private; but nothing is private.
Hundreds of strangers lie breathing around us
Wakeful, or coughing; or in sleep tossing;
Hundreds of strangers pressing upon us
Like horses tethered, tied to a manger.

My mother lies wakeful with her eyes staring.
I cannot see her, but I know. She is thinking:
This is a nightmare. She is back in her home
Embroidering blossoms on a silk kimono
Talking to me of Yosh (the boy I mentioned,
The one I grew up with). She is making plans
To visit the go-between; to bake for a wedding.

My mother cannot believe her dream is over,
That she lies in a manger with her hands tethered.
So you will understand now, Susumu:
I have not been able to tell my mother.
It is hard for me to believe, myself,
How you said the words, how you spoke of a garden
Where my name, MARIKO, would be written in
    flowers....
I wonder where in the inner country
On what train far from this animal silence
This thick night stifling my heart, my nostrils—
Where like a rocket shooting between two planets
Have you flown, Susumu? Have you gone?

ANNOUNCER:

Between the fury and the fear
The window-breaking rabble and the politician's
    blackout,
(Wartime panic fed
On peacetime provocations)
Between the curfew rung
On Powell Street
And the rows of bunks in a public stable

Between the line-ups and the labels and the presentation
    of a one-way ticket
Between these, and the human heart—
There was in every centre one man, a white man—
A minister, a layman—a mayor.

THE MAYOR:

That year the snow came early, lay lightly on our hills
Cooling their colours, pointing up the evergreen
Scribbled over the ledges; at valley's end
Snow muffled with its mantle the gaunt shape,
The smokeless chimney of the copper smelter.

I stood on the station platform reading the message
Telegraphed from Vancouver: 'The first contingent,
Sixty-eight persons, arriving on the night train.'
Then I looked down our narrow, funnelled valley
My ghost-town village, with hotels closed up
Since gold-rush days; post office perched
Upon a down-hill lurch, leaning toward empty store.

At seven-fifteen the evening train pulled in.
I stood alone on the platform, waiting.
Slowly the aliens descended, in huddled groups,
Mothers and crying children; boys and girls
Holding a bundle of blankets, cardboard boxes,
A basket of pots and pans, a child's go-cart—
Looking bewildered up and down the platform,
The valley closing in, the hostile village....

I stepped forward, urged into sudden action.
The women cowered, fell back, cried words
In panic to the old men standing surly, helpless.
I collared a young kid, bright, with his eyes snapping:
'You there, you speak English?' 'Why, yah! You bet.'
We eyed each other, and I smiled. 'You see,'
I said, 'I'm mayor here...your mayor.
This is your home. Can you tell the people that?
Tell them I'm here to meet them, get acquainted,

Find a place for them to sleep.' The boy
Nodded. 'Okay, I'll tell my mother, sure.
The rest will believe whatever she says to do.'

Their conference began. I waited, tense;
Then plunged into the job of lifting crates
And scanty furnishings, getting local lads
To pile it up on trucks; until I felt
A timid touch upon my arm; I turned
And saw the Issei mother.
                                        Putting out my hand
I felt hers move, rest for a moment in mine—
Then we were free. We began to work together....

ANNOUNCER:

These were the fathers, mothers, those
Who had to choose another home, another way.
What would they choose? The questioner
Paused with his pencil lifted; gave them a day
To talk together, choose.

THE WIFE:

Either to be a ghost in mountain towns
Abandoned by the seekers after gold,
There to sit with idle hands,
Embroidering the past upon a window-pane
Fed on foreign food
And crowded together in government huts
The men torn from our arms, the family parted,
Or to face the longer, stranger journey
Over the mountain ranges, barred from the sea—
To labour in uncertain soil, inclement weather
Yet labour as one—all the family together?

THE HUSBAND:

We looked at each other, you and I, after
So many doubtful years binding our struggles:

177

Our small plot grown to wider green
Pastured within the Fraser's folds, the shack
Upbuilded to a cottage, now a house—
The cherry trees abloom and strawberry fields
White with the snow of blossom, of promise.

THE WIFE:

Had it all to be done again, worked at again
By our gnarled hands, in a harsh new land
Where summer passes like a quick hot breath
And winter holds you chained for half the year?
You took my hands, and said: 'It's the children's country.
Let them choose.' They chafed for independence
Scenting the air of freedom in far fields.
Therefore we had no choice, but one straight way:
The eastward journey into emptiness,
A prairie place called home.

THE HUSBAND:

It was harder than hate. Home was a blueprint only.
We lived in a hen coop perched on a farmer's field
Soaked by the sudden storms, the early rains of April.
Yet there was time for ploughing, time to sow
Beet seed upon the strange black soil in rows
Of half an acre; we saw in neighbouring fields'
Bleak tableland, the stabbing green
Of the young wheat; and heard the sweet
Heart-snaring song of meadow-larks; in grass
Withered and brown saw maps move, empty patches
Purple with crocus underneath our feet.

In summer the sun's beak
Tore at our backs bending over the rows
Endless for thinning; the lumpy soil left callouses
Upon our naked knees; mosquitoes swarmed
In frenzied choruses above our heads
Sapping the neck; until a hot wind seared
The field, drove them away in clouds.

THE WIFE:

I think we had nearly given up, and wept
And gone for government help, another home —
Until, one evening lull, work done
You leaned upon the poplar gate to watch
A lime green sky rim the mauve twilight
While in the pasture fireflies danced
Like lanterns of Japan on prairie air.

Leaning the other way spoke our new friend
The neighbour from the Ukraine;
Touching your arm, using words more broken
Than yours, like scraps of bread left over.

'See how tomorrow is fine. You work
Hard, same as me. We make good harvest time.'
He came from a loved land, too, the mild
Plains of the Dneiper where, in early spring
(He said) the violets hid their sweetness. 'This land
Is strange and new. But clean and big
And gentle with the wheat. For children too,
Good growing.'
He lifted up his hands, his praise; we heard
Over the quickening fields a fresh wind blowing.

ANNOUNCER:

This one was young; but he wanted the world
For others. A philosopher,
He accepted the blow, Pearl Harbor.
He learned the way of waiting.

THE PHILOSOPHER:

To be alone is grace; to see it clear
Without rancour; to let the past be
And the future become. Rarely to remember
The painful needles turning in the flesh.

179

(I had looked out of the schoolroom window
And could not see the design, held dear
Of the shaken maples; nor the rain, searing and the stinging
The burning rain in the eye.

I could not see, nor hear my name called:
Tatsuo, the Pythagoras theorem!
I could not think till the ruler rapped
On the desk, and my mind snapped.

The schoolroom faded, I could not hold
A book again in my hand.
It was the not knowing; the must be gone
Yet the continual fear of going.

Yes, to remember is to go back; to take
The path along the dyke, the lands of my uncle
Stretching away from the river—
The dykeside where we played

Under his fruit tress, canopied with apples,
Falling asleep under a hedgerow of roses
To the gull's shrill chatter and the tide's recurrent
Whisper in the marshland that was home....)

So must I remember. It cannot be hid
Nor hurried from. As long as there abides
No bitterness; only the lesson learned
And the habit of grace chosen, accepted.

CHORUS OF NISEIS:

Home, we discover, is where life is:
Not Manitoba's wheat
Ontario's walled cities
Nor a B.C. fishing fleet.

Home is something more than harbour—
Than father, mother, sons;

Home is the white face leaning over your shoulder
As well as the darker ones.

Home is labour, with the hand and heart,
The hard doing, and the rest when done;
A wider sea than we knew, a deeper earth,
A more enduring sun.

Comrade

Once only did I sleep with you;
A sleep and love again more sweet than I
Have ever known; without an aftertaste.
It was the first time; and a flower could not
Have been more softly opened, folded out.
Your hands were firm upon me: without fear
I lay arrested in a still delight—
Till suddenly the fountain in me woke.

My dear, it's years between; we've grown up fast
Each differently, each striving by itself.
I see you now a grey man without dreams,
Without a living, or an overcoat:
But sealed in struggle now, we are more close
Than if our bodies still were sealed in love.

New Jersey: 1935

In the landlady's garden
we walked entwined in moonlight
Luella and I
tree and shadow of tree
linked white and black.
It was a time
before this present darkness
before flashes of violence
tore clouds with lighting crack—
but in the moonlight
we were visible
walking the landlady's garden
we were seen entering her house
climbing upstairs for supper.
And when Luella had left
(at least she waited till I closed the door)
the landlady shoved her shoulder
into mine
    and her frog eyes
into my face:
"Was that a coloured girl you dared to bring
into my home?"
"Why, yes, a social worker;
we have jobs together in the Settlement House."
"For that I could whack
the liver out of anyone. Don't ever
let a nigger enter my door again."
"Why no!—I never will—
not a white girl, either."
And I went upstairs
to pack.
They say it's the same thing, now
even in the North, the same
animal fear, frog eyes—
and in response

the same dark guttural laugh:
"You jest don' understand things, honey."

And I guess I don't understand
for I haven't been back.

The Fallow Mind

The fallow mind in winter knows, its scope
And wide horizon are made narrow by
The rim of early dusk, descending blinds—
Last summer's rocket buried under sand.
To soar and spin, to take the hand and whip
A leash of fiery comets through the sky:
To be crier or prophet, John or Isaiah, these
Wait in the mind for the world's turning phase:
The time she lifts her head from blood-soaked fields,
From one-eyed houses, shattered, gaping towns,
The time she sees her brother sun, and bares
Her ribs to his remembered healing blaze—
Then will the mind take a new stature on
And children thrive, who late last year were bombed.

The Child Looks Out

The child looks out from doors too high and wide for him
On words spun large as suns, huge meanings sprayed on
    tree
And roadway, spreading fields, not to be caught and
    clapped
Together in a rosy nave, the sun no coin
For fingers to indent.
                    The child runs out to stare
At masterful young men who bat a tennis ball
At giants in kilt skirts whose march is purposeful
At mothers in cool gowns who move about like moons
Upon the eternal lawns, low laughter shimmering
About their curving mouths.
                    The child leans on the future,
Slender tree ungainly rooted there by private worlds
Who knew a private ecstasy unshared by him
But let the memory slip and reared a hedge
Of bristling phrases, last year's bills, and week-ends
    snatched
In secret hate; his room laid waste when radios
Are tuned, when rumour's blatant voice hits nerve,
Dries tissue, brittles down
The new unmoulded bone.
                    The child in cities toddling up
A stifling reach of stair, gains window-seat:
How consternation puckers up his eyes—at space
Unplanted, seed unwanted, wars unwarranted
Consuming his small, thankless growing place!

Autumn: 1939

In our time the great ones fade
We hear the whisper of their falling
Words on a radio announce
How Yeats and Freud within a year
Heard the insistent silence calling.

In our time torpedoes score
In thunder-foam the ships go under
Blood is spurted from the sky
Ashes smoke where children played—
Gardens, pavements, split in plunder.

In our time no great ones live
For ears are censored from their singing—
No surgeon of the mind can touch
Pillar of salt, idiot stare
Bell-tongues meaninglessly swinging.

Spain

When the bare branch responds to leaf and light
Remember them: it is for this they fight.
It is for haze-swept hills and the green thrust
Of pine, that they lie choked with battle dust.

You who hold beauty at your finger-tips
Hold it because the splintering gunshot rips
Between your comrades' eyes; hold it across
Their bodies' barricade of blood and loss.

You who live quietly in sunlit space
Reading The Herald after morning grace
Can count peace dear, when it has driven
Your sons to struggle for this grim, new heaven.

In Time of War

You went, wordless; but I had not the will
Nor courage to find fanciful or plumaged phrase
To camouflage my solitude. So saying bald
Good-bye, word bouncing down each waiting step
Till out of sight and sound, I saw you turn
Walk firm toward the iron gate. Its clang
Shattered a world. For should we greet again
This hushed horizon will have widened so
You'll not find solace walking in the Park
Or watching storm snarl over English Bay.
That night of fog, bleaching the bones of trees
Will not shroud you and me again; too wide apart
We will have grown; our thoughts too proud
Too tall for sheltering beneath these boughs.

V-J Day

It seemed a poor thing to do, to wed, when the Japanese
Had begun to gnaw their way through the Manchu
    plains,
When Spain cast a ballot, and was outraged, raped
In an olive grove, by a monastery wall.
It seemed no time for love, when the hands
Idled in empty pockets and coffee was five cents a cup.
It seemed no time to lie down in a clearing
At sundown, with the woodcutters gone, and the thrush's
Voice fluting the firs. But you said: "Have faith."
You said, "Only Hitler was in a hurry and his haste
Would one day be spent." So you said. And we wed.
Now it is eight years after, to the day, to the hour:
The wrath has devoured itself and the fire eaten the fire.
And again at sundown over the bird's voice, low
Over the firs fluted with evening I hear the Yangtse flow
And the rubble of Barcelona in this moss under my hand.

Improvisation on an Old Theme

If I must go, let it be easy, slow
The curve complete, and a sure swerve
To the goal. Let it be slow and sweet
To know how leaf consumes its time,
How petal sucks to the sun's heat
Or as old bones, settling into soil,
Eyes too remote for earth's light
Set on a solar circle whose bright
Business brims the universe.

Let me know well how the winds blow
Smoky in autumn with leaf reek;
And summer's sleek surrender,
Torching the maple; let my branches sigh
For snow, and in a muffled mantle, let me go.

Keep me for quiet. Save me ever from
Disastrous ending sounding without drum,
No decent exhalation of the breath—
The dazzling violence of atomic death.

After Hiroshima

Not any more the visions and revelations
A voice at Emmaus, a figure of light on the hills;
Not any more the courtesan running early
To pray, and the prayer answered in act: an
    astonished tomb.

We see no mysteries; miracles are not accepted,
The beating rain bears no messages for man;
Though sun may still burn hot, searing the skin
No hearts dare listen while fear stirs the womb.

What the right hand doeth, stirring the pot of evil—
The hydrogen brew; the left knows not, is sleeping;
If the mind asserts, the heart dare not conjecture;
The picture upon the wall is unveiled, but dare not
    speak.

Not any more the visions and revelations:
Only in brief flashes is light received, good news.
Only a child's belief, rocked in a cradle of doubt,
Can prophesy our safety; illuminate our hope.

The Poetry

In the past I have frowned upon poets who write about their art—often instead of living it. Yet, as I muse through my collections, I find there are many poems that deal with the creative experience—whether it is poured into poetry, music, painting, or sculpture. The interplay between the arts and the "pull" of changing forms, revised cultural myths, create in themselves fascinating poetic subjects.

Surrealism, imagism, lyricism, may come and go. So what wind blows next? Pop art (or self-expression?) seems to have bounded into every global village.

Dream Sequence: I and II

I. Dream

Sudden
a sceptred bird
swept through the window
into the blue room
and dazzled me

I swam in light—
he stooped
and pecked out my eyes
>   I move in darkness now
>   fumbling the walls
>   trying to remember
>   blue
>   >   (I have closed the window
>   >   and the sun falls cold
>   >   though glass)

II. The Visitation

Through the bushes on my right
movement   branches bending
I saw a fluttering
animal?   bird?
Then it emerged
rose into air
flew over   hovering
great blue-grey bird
trailing a black tail
(so graceful)

Now she was beside me
tall as a young filly
letting me stretch out my hand
to stroke her feathery flanks—

How beautiful you are.
She turned her head:
Have you been married?
To a man, yes.
I mean: to a god…
Have you ever been married
to a god?
No.
Well then,   I can work with you.

And as I stroked her
she named two authors I should read
(but I couldn't visualize their names).

Message delivered
she flew off
in a whirl of wings.

Since when
my humming heart
sings

Inarticulate

Inarticulate
at the year's dying
what a wind,
what a voice crying!
(My throat's tight,
my heart on leash).

This is again November—
the time to remember
how the wind cries out
things people would not shout
nor whisper, even.
Things people dream about.

(On a still day—hush!
When gold leaves fell
I nearly told you
all there was to tell.

But something held me:
your look, a word—
my thought sank downward
before you heard.

Now, grown accustomed
to reticence:
I scarcely heed
what the wind flaunts).

What a wind!
What a voice crying.
What a wind and yet
somewhere my voice
between the drifts
of wind and leaf,
somewhere my voice—
Articulate?

Fire and Reason

I cannot shut out the night—
nor its sharp clarity.

The many blinds we draw,
you and I,
The many fires we light
can never quite obliterate
the irony of stars
the deliberate moon
the last, unsolved finality of night.

Sea-Flowers

Your thoughts must be the sea-flowers
Unstirred by any breeze
Whose only honey is the salt
Stored up by minnow bees.

Your thoughts that sway in water
Beyond the arm of light
Are cold and waxen and remote,
Drift downward out of sight.

Thus, though they be eternal,
Unheeding suns or snows
I choose the trembling flower of earth
That breathes before it goes.

Lorca

for Federico Garcia Lorca*

When veins congeal
And gesture is confounded
When pucker frowns no more
And voice's door
Is shut forever

On such a night
My bed will shrink
To single size
Sheets go cold
The heart hammer
With life-loud clamour
While someone covers up the eyes.

Ears are given
To hear the silence driven in
Nailed down.
And we descend now down from heaven
Into earth's mould, down.

> *While you—*
> *You hold the light*
> *Unbroken.*

When you lived
Day shone from your face:
Now the sun rays search
And find no answering torch.

If you were living now
This cliffside tree
And its embracing bough
Would speak to me.

*Spanish poet, shot, it was said, by Franco's men.

197

If you were speaking now
The waves below
Would be the organ stops
For breath to blow.

And if your rigid head
Flung back its hair
Gulls in a sickle flight
Would circle there.

> *You make the flight*
> *Unshaken.*

You are alive!
O grass flash emerald sight
Dash of dog for ball
And skipping rope's bright blink
Lashing the light!

High in cloud
The sunset fruits are basketed
and fountains curl their plumes
On statue stone.
In secret thicket mould
Lovers defend their hold,
Old couples hearing whisperings
Touch in a handclasp, quivering.

For you sang out aloud
Arching the silent wood
To stretch itself, tiptoe,
Above the crowd...

> *You hold the word*
> *Unspoken.*

You breathe. You be.
Bare, stripped light
Time's fragment flagged
Against the dark.

You dance. Explode
Unchallenged through the door
As bullets burst
Long deaths ago, your heart.

And song outsoars
The bomber's range
serene with wind-
Manoeuvred cloud.

Light flight and word
The unassailed, the token!

For The New Year

Stamped in the throat
bird song
biologists say
is inevitable
as that beak   that eye
that red wing
is not *learned*
is born with the bird

Perhaps then there's another
dimension behind our learned
word patterns...
perhaps an infinite song
sways in our throats
yet to be heard?

Fantasia

for Helena Coleman, Toronto poet

And I have learned how diving's done
How breathing air, cool wafted trees
Clouds massed above the man-made tower
How these
Can live no more in eye and ear:
And mind be dumb
To all save Undine and her comb.

Imagination's underworld: where child goes down
Light as a feather. Water pressure
Hardly holds him, diving's easy
As the flight of bird in air
Or bomber drumming to his lair.

Child goes down, and laughingly
(He's not wanted yet, you see)
Catches fishes in his hand
Burrows toe in sifting sand
Seizes all the weeds about
To make a small sub-rosa boat
Then up he bobs, as easily
As any blown balloon
To greet the bosky, brooding sky
And hunger for the sun.

*

And child grown taller, clothed in man's
Long limbs, and shaggy hair, his chin outthrust
Searches for years the rounded world
Climbs to its peaks, falls to its valleys green
Striding the trim and trailing towns
Fingering the fond arteries

Possessing things, and casting them
Cloakwise to earth for sleeping time…

Sometime the lust wanderer
Will sleep, will pause; will dream of plunging deep
Below it all, where he will need
No clock companion, thorn in flesh, no contact man
To urge him from the ground.
For flying's easy, if you do it diving
And diving is the self unmoored
Ranging and roving—man alone.

*

And I have learned how diving's done
Wherefore the many, many
Chose the watery stair
Down, down Virginia
With your fêted hair
Following after Shelley
Or wordcarvers I knew
(Bouchette; and Raymond, you)—
Here is the fascination
Of the salty stare:
And death is here.
Death courteous and calm, glass-smooth
His argument so suave, so water-worn
A weighted stone.
And death's deliberation, his
Most certain waiting-room
His patience with the patient, who will be
His for infinity…

So no astounded peerers
On the surface craft
No dragging nets, no cranes
No gnarled and toughened rope
Not any prayer nor pulley man-devised
Will shake the undersea
Or be

More than a brief torpedo, children's arrow
More than a gaudy top outspun
Its schedule done...

*

Wise to have learned: how diving's done
How breathing air, cool wafted trees
Clouds massed above the man-made tower
How these
Can live no more in eye and ear:
And mind be dumb
To all save Undine and her comb...

Without Benefit of Tape

The real poems are being written in outports
on backwoods farms
in passageways where pantries still exist
or where geraniums
nail light to the window
while out of the window boy in the flying field
is pulled to heaven on the keel of a kite.

Stories breed in the north:
men with snow in their mouths
trample and shake at the bit
kneading the woman down under blankets of snow
icing her breath, her eyes.

The living speech is shouted out
by men and women leaving railway lines
to trundle home, pack-sacked
just company for deer or bear—

    Hallooed
across the counter, in a corner store
it booms upon the river's shore:
on midnight roads where hikers flag you down
speech echoes from the canyon's wall
    resonant
    indubitable.

The Incendiary

for Duncan

Now that the poetry's bursting out
all over the place
firecrackers setting off explosions
under train wheels
bombs
under hydrants
"bloody marvellous"
I can hear you saying
your eyes bulging and blazing
with that flinty excitement

as if every bone in your body
though burnt now   to ashes
had started a conflagration
had gone off crackling
and shooting poems
all over the bloody map
Canada—

      country you came to, late
      and loved with hate
      and longed to set fire to

For Abe Klein: Poet

and lives alone, and in his secret shines
like phosphorous. At the bottom of the sea.
A.M.K.

Drowned? Were you the one
drowned
or do I dream again
and do I hold your hand across a table
in a Chinese restaurant
Leo and Art gesticulating chopsticks?
Hand reaching to affirm
against the goyish laughter?

A drowned man now ... Your hand
that delicate instrument
long servant to
the fervent ferment of thought
your hand lies twitching out
a spider's mark
on the bare table

And in the hive, your head
the golden bowl
bees buzz and bumble
fumble for honey amidst empty cells
where the slain poems
wingless, tremble.

ii

Break down the twigs, break down the boughs
But break not, Lord, the golden bowl.
A.M.K.

My body is tree
my reaching boughs and twigs

are skeleton
meant to be
broken by stone
by shouldering snow
splintered by rain
cracked by the fingering frost

My body is given, Lord
to show Thy ways
I read where my roots go
assess the green
count leaves' ascension
into heaven's blaze

This will I willingly
submit to Thee:
my skeleton,
my tree.

iii

He breaks the wineglass underneath his heel.
A.M.K.

When they come
as they will come
the marching men
with kaftan and phylactery
mounting the stairs

And when your ears
hear for the last time
those long Kaddish prayers

(You lying in bed
in the next room
lone)
Pray
not with those Hebrew words
pray the winged praise he made

in English
on your wedding night
Singing the bride and all the seven days.

iv

> The wrath of people is like foam and lather
> Risen against us. Wherefore, Lord, and why?
>
> A.M.K.

Tender the boy's song
and honey sweet
the Kantor's hymn
(Loud the descending beast
devouring them)

Fair, in the circling light
the 'green inventory'
of field and wood
the mother shielding
her in-yearning
outward-yielding brood.

But dark in the river's bed
the coiled sequestered shape
reared up, and spewed
his lava black
lather of hate.

Making the Poem

for Jack Spicer,
before his death

                i

 Dreams are just
                furniture
Jack said
Like words you keep pushing around
till they fit into the room
                        somehow
I begin
        at the beginning

                ii

Dreams are
                personalities
the eight sides of your head
shifting in sunlight
but dreams do not reveal
        they obscure

                iii

The serial poem is a
                        progression
not a repetition
a movement
                breaking through
                        outwards
splashing the shore
the swimmer heaves himself upwards
onto a rock
                far from the highway

iv

I wake:
it's middle of night, danger
is the poem. Here
it's been waiting, counting, am I
ready?

v

Terror
terror at the white line
            strain
never to finish
                    (don't let me finish)
there are
an infinitude   of   finishes
miracles
are a way out

Pyllis, Reading Her Poems

What would it be like? she muses
to have the name Wah
and thereby, for non-Chinese readers
achieve namelessness?
No connotations.

A juggler, she pulls out cards
anonymous thoughts
and throws them five at a time
into the air
then presto
catches them
in her nimble-witted fingers
calls them
examines the significance
addresses herself to
relationships
and smiling a Chinese smile
lays them down on the desk
into restless rest.

Wunderbar

for Almuth, sculptor

How you reach into
the *joie de vivre*
le vif   le vivace   et le bel aujourd'hui
climbing   soaring   exPLODING
How you do this
is a kind of miracle
a blessing—
the laying on of hands

Your hands   manipulating
earth's essence   clay
pouring it on   cleaning it off
till the transformation
shines forth

How you do it
you do not know
nor ploughing through these furrows
of words
do I

Picasso, Sketching

He lays his lines, blaspheming rules' precision,
silver and black converging, juxtaposed,
angles colliding, parallels enclosed:
distorts perspective, daggers the bull's eye
and then, his cornucopia conjured from thin air
tossed to a corner, dazzles out a scrawl—
Hen's track? Hen's eggs? Hen's teeth? They purl
and plane; ripple and pearl to grey again.

Il faut risquer tout!
Smoke from a tunnel belches cumulus,
the rearing engine truckles to its tracks,
snorts to a pause; develops eyes and nose,
is Taurus-teased, insanely furious.
Busy the fingers fly to tame it down
seizing the rein and haltering the frown
then easing to its customary stance—
Et voilà, ça m'amuse!
Stationed but champing, belching fire and fuss.

So does he shunt his visions through the station,
sets dynamite in open air, ignites creation.

Bartok and the Geranium

She lifts her green umbrellas
Towards the pane
Seeking her fill of sunlight
Or of rain;
Whatever falls
She has no commentary
Accepts, extends,
Blows out her furbelows,
Her bustling boughs;

And all the while he whirls
Explodes in space,
Never content with this small room:
Not even can he be
Confined to sky
But must speed high and higher still
From galaxy to galaxy,
Wrench from the stars their momentary notes
Steal music from the moon.

She's daylight
He is dark
She's heaven-held breath
He storms and crackles
Spits with hell's own spark.

Yet in this room, this moment now
These together breathe and be:
She, essence of serenity,
He in a mad intensity
Soars beyond sight

Then hurls, lost Lucifer
From heaven's height.

And when he's done, he's out:
She leans a lip against the glass
And preens herself in light.

Sleeping In Sally's Library

As I awake
from a dream of holding a baby
a thousand voices call down from the shelves:
Hear me! Hear me!

As I grow more alert
feeling the windowed sunlight
on my eyes
old whiffs of song
sound in my ears:

le vierge le vivace et le bel aujourd'hui
where the nights are long
Quand je serai bien vielle
when I am old and grey and full of sleep.

Nella sua voluntade e nostra pace
when in disgrace with fortune and men's eyes—

These are my voices of reply.
Hear me. Stay on that shelf.
Stay closed.
I am vibrating with your messages.

Nocturne

for Alan Crawley

Countries are of the mind
and when you moved upon my land
your darkness ringed my light:
O landscape lovely, looped
with loping hills, wind-woven
landfall of love.

All my frozen years
snow drifting through bare birches
white-cowled cedar
and the black stream threading through ice —

All sultry summer run
barefooted through the crackling wood
flung upon rocks made skeleton
x-rayed by the raging sun —

All springs, wild crying with the wood's mauve bells
anemone, hepatica
breast against bark, the sap's ascent
burning the blood with bold green fire —

All autumns, solitary season
treading the leaves, treading the time:
autumns that stripped deception to the bone
and left me animal, alone —

All seasons were of light
stricken and blazing —
Only now the shout
of knowledge hurls, amazing:
O bind me with ropes of darkness,
bind me with your long night.

The Second Language

for Raphael

i

We walk between words
as if they were trees
touching rough bark
exploring origins.
Linked, in this green shade
a tree's name shadows us
I share its history
with you
who came
a first man to this forest.
And you find roots
you look uncurls each leaf
till every word we speak
thrusts upwards from its mother dark
and sparks our eyes with light.

ii

Now in our black
forest
moonlight fructifies
leaves go silver:
soundless shadows,
the trees parade
star-pierced
in a blue light.

iii

How to examine heaven
how with naked eye
outstare fierce stars?

Our words are torn to shreds
by the shrill cicadas.
We turn away—
the wanting mouth
closed
the longing arms
clamped.

iv

If in the dark
I stumbled against your mouth
would my arms stay pinned
at my back—
                or shiver forward
                    white flowering
                        into black?

v

And in between night's sheets
imagined conversations flower
more real
than day's   disjointed
sentences

And when lips seal
and sleep takes over
myth and irrelevance of dream
are drawn
a dark cover

vi

Then who shall blame the dagga smoker?
the madman who escapes in terror?
the drummer beating out his warning?
I also   also you
enter into league with these:
by you and me

(who do not dare to speak)
are such deeds done:
we suffer
and do not condone
we wait our turn.

Precautions

Not to be tied
to time
today's newspapers
tucked under the bed
any time   any day
and then
it's always the same
No settlement
but scuttlement
No rain
but drought
No oranges
from South Africa
(the wine also
never bought)
Oranges   oranges
"Navels, my dear"
"Delicious"
Buy   Buy   Buy
and kill every other child
at Soweto

The Dismembered Poem

Because in a moment of thaw
the poem saw light
was nailed on a café wall
chanted at night

It is now required to recant
to recapture the words
flown out into air
faster than summer birds.

What matter if song be condemned
declared null and void
torn limb from limb
dismembered, destroyed?

The words like seeds exist
declare themselves in air
behind walls, on the hidden ear
under the crack of the door

Around a fire, in the gloom
sombre the faces gaze
then flare at the words flung out
from memory's blaze.

Recant! Recant! that cry
is only a public noise:
behind the door in the dark
affirms the exultant voice.

Two Lives*

Pat
    believed in the new world
           for woman   man   and child
    was murdered
           by her husband
    hammered on head
           with an axe

Sharon
    believed in the new world
           for woman   man   and child
    but murdered
    herself
           (were they dream-besot
             or star-guided?)

Who will now speak for them
           as poets
these two who lived by the wonder
           of the word
Who will stand up
           and be counted
for their sake
will stay alive
womanning the last barricade
till the end of falsehood?

*Pat Lowther (1935-1975) published three collections of poetry—
This Difficult Flowering (1968), *The Age of the Bird* (1972), and *Milk
Stone* (1974)—during her lifetime; two others have appeared
posthumously: *A Stone Diary* (1977) and *Final Instructions* (1980).

Sharon Stevenson (1946-1978) published one book of poems, *Stone*
(1972). A selection of her published and unpublished work
appeared under the title *Gold Earrings* in 1984.

The Emperor's Circus

(on seeing his drawings reproduced)

They called him cold   recalcitrant
old   in a dying court
he put
duty before grace
was to himself
unmerciful
          Franz Josef
imperator   impersonal

          Only a name;
          once it was plain Franz
          and he fifteen,
          learning now to dance
          taken by tutor to
          the Cirque français
          to see the acrobats
          watch horses prance.
          Pulling his pencil out
          his laughter caught the tumbler's leap
          the circus master, elegant with whip
          the acrobats half taken by surprise
          mastering the air
          and centred on each page
          he drew the horses, tossing manes
          the tremor of their hoofs, the cries
          of innocent creatures circling the dust:
          he saw the silence
          yielding in their eyes.

Alone upon an empty throne
the old man frowned:
setting his house to rights
his papers in their proper place
he saw mild horses leaping
in that land once captured by his lines—
and could not bring himself
to rip the pages, feed the flames

but tossed them into time.

Poetry Is Like Bread

Poetry is like bread
Neruda said
It should be shared
by everyone

We women are everyone
beginning to share
Poetry is communication
not a game
played with words:
a poem is a message

> Listen to the morning's birds
> signalling delight
> at noon their startled warnings
> change to song at evening
> soothing the feathers down

> Regard the fir trees
> how they group
> together talk
> When enemies descend
> in catapulting swarms
> know how the trees
> change chemistry
> to banish the worms

Our poem—everyone's—
must be   a message
for survival
Let it sound out clear
signpost and banner
plain talk:

NO MORE WAR

Tale

for Malcolm Lowry

It was not the lock that disturbed—for I had the key
But over the lock, that web of filigree
And the large black witch who watched
From her wheel house, so intricately latched.

Some might have taken warning, gone away
Up sodden path, through evergreen
Past devil's club and spleen
Dashed into daylight and the hard highway

But I took the key, fitted it into lock
And turned. The spider house split loose,
Witch scuttled off to hide, fell prey
For the intruder's foot, the stranger's way.

So did I come to own that hen-legged house,
And the house, surprised, grew meeker than a
    mouse.

Malcolm, I wrote some poems here for you
Defying all black magic: hear me, hold me true.

Lament And Praise

for Peter Tempest*

To enter in
the door is language
You opened it wide
as if on roller skates
you soared through
into the songs of Pushkin
Achmatova   loved woman
Vaptsarov   Bulgarian Hero
rendering their words
into words of English

Feverish almost
indefatigable
how you gloried in work—
translation for its own sake?
Sometimes   old-fashioned lapses
the cliché rhyme
But poet yourself,
you sought to turn the overcoat
inside out
and reveal that Russian lining

Some failures   some
brilliant insights
for you opened the door
of our narrow world
to shout the planets' secrets

*Translator, died suddenly in Moscow, July 1985.

The House of Winter

for Anna Achmatova

> As though the tears I wept myself
> I drank from another's cupped hands
> —A.A.

Now I begin to put my house in order
but thinking   dreaming
only of you:
How you were twenty when I was born
How you lived through the revolution
when I was a child unknowing, unknown—
But the house of winter was our home:
You, on the Neva
I, on Assinaboine
Afterwards our lives crossed
across distances
weaving the crucifixions
women learn how to suffer—
and yet, in 1935 I nearly took flight
for Leningrad and Tsarskoe Selo.
Now, reading your Requiem
I know the pain I was spared
I know the prison doors you beat upon
that I never faced.
Marriage and children turned me away
from friends and comrades jailed
and their confinement was not torture
in my country:
only frustration and boredom

At Hiroshima
thought stopped
Peace became War
words were pebbles
flung into deep water

And now I have seen Leningrad and Moscow
I, from Winnipeg and Montreal
and by saying your words slowly
nose buried in an armful of flowers
by naming your signposts:
bird   snow   willow   stone

Now I am stalwart
can ready myself
to believe in you
as person, poet, woman—
I cry *Arise again!*
I cry with my hands groping
hands that seek
to cover you with love

At the Finish

Greater minds than mine have coped with the philosophical problems of living and dying. My comments on these subjects are, at best, tentative, and at worst gloomy—not to be taken seriously but to be appreciated as one pulls up the blind, longing for clear skies and delighted when they happen.

One rides on through the tunnel, seeing light.

What light? Does it matter? The great goal should be to celebrate along the way song and dance, youth and age. For in growing older there lies the possibility of affirmation: seeing younger.

Ice Age

In this coming cold
devouring our wheat fields
and Russia's
there'll be no shadow
nor sign of shadow
all cloud, shroud
endless rain
eternal snow

In this coming cold
which we have fashioned
out of our vain jet-pride,
the supersonic planes
will shriek destruction
upon the benign
yin yang
ancient and balanced universe

Worse than an animal
man tortures his prey
given sun's energy
and fire's blaze
he has ripped away
leaf
    bird
        flower
is moving to destroy
the still centre
heart's power.

Now who among us
will lift a finger
to declare *I am of God, good?*
Who among us
dares to be righteous?

Aging

My body haunts me
thieves in on me at night
shattering sleep
with nameless pointless pains

Where do you ache?
The Chinese doctor's skill
might poise with needle
over my tossing form

but there's no
one still spot   no
one still time I'd swear:
The pain is here.

And every night
my fingers search the wound, the old
spine curvature, the creaking knees...
but tongues, the darting tongues
lick elsewhere, fan desire
until all yesterdays are gulfed
in freezing fire.

News From Nootka

for Louis Frank, Ahausit

They say the Tibetan monks came here
centuries past
wiped their feet on our shore—
In the roots of cedars
left silverware and prayers
walked into ocean
with incantations, ablutions
in praise of sunrise.

If it were all surmise
I'd be less shaken
than now, seeing you
strong, serene
priest of the cedars
figure emerging from argellite
sure-footed on the rock shore
launching canoes for fishing…
"When we had enough
we gave the rest to the village."

Something of how you were taken
into the troughs of the ocean
riding upon it alone
all night long
"in the dark a man is so small, so small"
Something about the spray shaken
out of your hair
and the calm brow
assure me now
the ancient messages endure:

"Receive me, O Maker of Morning
ready to act for my people."

Raven laid the sun in your lap:
your mind caught fire.

Widow

The woman remembering
the man who died
that sweet connection
the woman sowing
nasturtium seed
planting geraniums
feels, waking at midnight
flowers growing out of her belly
rain falling on her thighs
the itch of nipples
pouting for kisses

The woman remembering
uses her hand to thrust
tries to recover
the heave and wrestle

but knows
it's all play
and games
knows how memory
can never seal
that bond of flesh
body within body

The Cabbage

The doctor goes on handing out pills
that reduce me
from animal
to vegetable

Why couldn't he
implant some sunflower seeds
so at least I'd be able to see
over the fence?

Mathematics

I want to play the great game, darling
but only you can play it to perfection:
Much talk..no bed.   Some talk.. some bed
no talk..all bed;   and talk tomorrow.

I meant to play the great game, darling
and hold your bones deep to the root of one
I meant to play the great game, darling
but the heart for it   is gone.

For Rent

People have to live, I know that
explained the old Scotch body
from the rooms next door:
If they have a cough
they have to cough!
I can take that

but people don't have to shout all night
and play judo on the floor
so I can't get a stitch
of sleep

It's not people's morals I'm complaining about
… I know all about birds beasts and flowers …
that's not my business

It's how they don't care about the walls
and the creaking floors
and the paint falling down from the ceiling
onto my good rug

And I can't pay anymore rent
than this

I've got nowhere to go.

The Dark House

It is as if we had gashed the wood
splintered the tree
sawed waves in half
battered at ice
broken that glassy
sea

It is as if
we had rallied   conspired
to destroy our lives
the space
where we breathed

It is as if we were born
to tear earth apart
and turned ourselves
into that dark energy
emerging   where?
black eyes blinking
unable to see
any solution
clear

It is as if we were born to deny life
cut throats
gasp for a spasm of air
then end it
there

It is as if
we were not meant
to be here

The Other Side Of The Wall

for Pat Page

I have climbed
put my foot in the rock
looked over.
That tangled secret garden
weedful, with fallen trees
thistles and thrusting flowers
is not fearsome...
would welcome a clean-up
a lover.

Beyond, sky is serene
song lulls the air
all things once living have changed
but live on
there.

The wall is death.
My death. Not to be climbed
yet.
I have no fear.

Thumbing A Ride

I am the one who receives the many
cars coming at me:
I am the one
they are the many in familied boxes
flying for picnics
or in twos, man driving
woman slouched sleepwise

I am the one
glued standing
hand raised in a quick uncertain gesture
without a machine to run me
or animal to ride on
two legs for walking two eyes for talking
the sun sinking fast...
and beside this bare highway
only ditch grasses
bulrush frogsong
kildeer's grounded nest

I am the one desperate
to shout my predicament
passed by these hundreds
whizzing fast forward
to fixed destinations
I am unfixed
but glued to the highway
and even the kildeer
cries out against me
for invading his kingdom
his wings fluttering and feinting above me
his wings bring him home

I am the one
alone on the highway
language exists
in my thumb

Bus Trip

(a found poem)

I'm an Indian
but I married a bohunk.
As soon as I git home
he gives me shit
and now I gotta git back
make his supper—
can't even fry an egg
he can't

Sure, he loves me
but I don't sleep with him
no more
gave him six kids
that's plenty—
now he's old too
and I say
what good's a bow
without the arrow?

I keep him as a spare—
when you go by car
you gotta have a spare!

Salute To Monty Python

What I dig is
reversals:
transvestites, almost
these 5 old ladies are
trans-generationists
who take on
the motorcycle gang
the hold-up guy
kidnappers and hi-jackers
and simply bomb the town
with the power of their ten arms.

Cheers.
to be over sixty
and running the show
with everybody scuttling
for cover.

I notice nobody
in the young audience
laughs
or is even faintly amused.
I am the only one
doubled up with mirth
(getting my own back?)

Let old age take over
with violence
ruthless possession
physical knockouts
if only to demonstrate
the other side of the mirror:
how *you* look to *us*
kiddos.

Interiors

I am sitting in another house
by another window
a green plaid blanket
over my knees

There is a garden outside..
trees..
grass sloping to the river
as far as the eye sees

It is summer and winter
fall and spring
all in one view
breath-catching

It is time to go
and time to come
children springing into men
and old men dwindling
into green

I am listening for your step
and when you come, I fling
all old age off
am in your arms
enveloped by that home

And then your face
is other faces found
your voice
is other voices
scaling a new sound

Then all are gone..

The trees bow down
the river rises up
crashing against the pane:
those waters swamp the room
and bear me on.

The Drive To Live

Half our life
spent in sleep—
how?   why?

I seek   (strange fugitive)
to seal the impression of the dream
People talking   talking
saying *what*?
Rarely it comes
is revealed
Rarely the joy on wakening
knowing what to do
now

So, are we only sent
to receive back our lives
in fragments?
No computer can reveal
my dreams
nor send me shooting
into the arms
of eternity
absolved

One Way Conversation

There are many men like you, perhaps
most certainly
most

but even though I've had
an itch for the seven-inch
reach   the hard entry
yet
I cannot despise you!

A woman wants above all
to be touched, caressed,
massaged and kissed
and what she carries away
the next day
is pride of flesh
love of link with man
human to human

O do not be distressed
that you cannot create
the great illusion:
thundering gods
at the womb's intrusion...
You have a role
valid as sunshine
of speech as equal
of man in parallel
pain... joy...
partner to woman
You have a role   gently caressing
human to human

The Survivor: Downed Pilot (Edmonton)

The body of the woman
devours me
her rigid flesh
frozen beside me in our cave
under the plane's wing
her body
takes on cold's contours
snow's soft hills
her eyes are pools of ice
staring skyward
if I put a match
to her white breasts
streams would surely run
her pure snow melting
into rivulets of wildness
wilderness silence.

I lie dreaming
of her body vanishing   vanished
into the firs and conifers
into the ice bound rock
her blood a gold vein
in the rock's granite

I lie dreaming
and hunger shakes me
I am faint
I move trembling
searching again for lichen   for wood
to light the fire
and boil snow with bark in it
for tea—
one more day and night
unfound
under the snapping cold
sky's vast glitter

One more night and day
and at evening
the woman haunts me
I lie down beside her
there's flame still
in the embers
I take it and brand
her thighs
I soften her buttocks with fire
my knife chops
I eat
later I will watch the blood
running down my fingers
and freezing

I light the fire again
three more nights
and the sky searchers
find us

> Now I work with the past
> tense
> my life is caught in the past
> net
> she lies beside me, melting
> but I freeze
> heart clangs
> stone in a body of stone
>
> the body of the woman I ate
> moves over me
> her mouth
> devours my mouth.

Return To A Birthplace

Hi lady   lady
ladybird
the children cry
as you sedately
walk waylaid

(when you are fifty
you don't feel any older
said the mother
brushing the pollen
from her shoulder)

fly away, fly away home

High lady   lady
feet first
gopher on the grass
then up, fly
tickle your toes
on tip-tops
of cottonwood
assess
the sky-blue
sea
with cloud sails scarfed
across the soil
where over the knuckles
of last year's cracks
and white whiskers of stubble
your tableland   spreads black...
Then let
new blades of wheat
grow a green fur
over the earth-bare
ribs

And fly!
on wings new grown
O lady   lady
skim high sky

When you come down
Where is your home?
Your house is on fire
Your children are gone.

Breathing

"You smell good
        you smell
as a woman should"

There have been eaters
    and drinkers of me
    painters of me
    eye bright
    and one singer
    who wreathed me
    in an aria

But I had yet to discover
    how even in old age
    a woman moves
    with freshness
is a leaf   perhaps
or a breath of wind
in a man's nostrils

On Seeing 'The Day of the Dolphin'

Years later
he might wander on that shore
aging and alone
longing not for wife
nor children grown
but for Alpha
'Fah' that dolphin
loved   cavorting

He might wander back and forth
kicking at sand   sharp   pebbles   shells
wishing to see that more vibrant
dance of life:
body action
ballet leap
from ocean
into ocean shelter
'going to English school'—
that squeaky dolphin shriek:
'Fah love Pa.'

Because of touch
loving survives
even amongst humans
always amongst dolphins

O rub my shoulders
stroke my finny skin!
convince me
I am next of kin

Arbutus

for Anthony

Wrapped in a storm
the tree crashed
onto the cliffside—
'garden sculpture' you said
and sawed through the grain

Those naked bones
stand upright now
leaning against the house
gleam white in moonlight
yellow in sunlight
or sea's delight
misted in rain
free from frost
winter's pain:
unliving—yet
in different form
alive!

We too, olding
cut off from roots
are part of the west's
seascape   landscape
our faces sculptured
into the garden wall
our voices lilting
near   far
through fronded forest
a part of frog song's
throbbed refrains

Not love now
but the memory of the tree
the memory of love
sustains

As We Grow Older

Perhaps it is
the intense and piercing grip
on another's person
the letting rip
of an ever creating tension—
till hypertension
slowly lessens
lets go

Passion is less
hate extinguishes itself
but what's left, and venerable
is bread-and-butter
brother-sister
talk across the table—
plain love!

The Artefacts: West Coast

In the middle of the night
I hear this old house breathing
a steady sigh
when oak trees and rock shadows
assemble silence
under a high
white moon

I hear the old house turn
in its sleep
shifting the weight of long dead footsteps
from one wall to another
echoing the children's voices
shrilly calling
from one room to the next

repeating those whispers in the master bedroom
a cry, a long sigh of breath
from one body to another
when the holy ghost takes over

In the middle of the night
I wake
and hear time speaking

First it was forest; rock;
hidden ups and downs
a hill where oaks and pines
struggled
and if a stranger climbed
the topmost pine
he'd see the ocean flattening the mountains
the forest, serried—
below, only the sculpted bays
native encampments
ceremonial lodges, totem poles
and winter dances
the Raven overall
giver-of-light, supervising
and the white whale imminent
evil lurking
to be appeased with ritual
long hair dancing
feathered masks

> *But history begins*

the woman said

> *when you are thirty*
> *that tomtom, time*
> *begins to beat*
> *to beat for you*

And in this city on the brink
of forest—sea—
history delights that Queen Victoria
made marriage with the totem wilderness

the cedar silences
the raven's wing

Now ravens build here still
seagulls spiral
the happy children in these attics
breathe and cry
unwittingly
the names of history
tumble from their lips:
Nootka   Nanaimo
Masset   Ucluelet
The map leaps up
>   *here did I live*
>   *was born and reared*
>   *here died*

So also said Chief Maquinna   Jewitt   Emily Carr
The map leaps up
from namelessness
to history
each place made ceremonial
when named
and its name
peopled!
events shouted!

>   *here the waters divided*
>   *here the whale bellowed*

In the middle of the night
the house heaves, unmoored
launched on a vast sea.

The Old Bawd

The men I loved
never recognized
my devotion

the men who loved me
never yielded
to my compassion

nor rocketed my body
into creation

The men I love now
are starved children

Windows

The way these plants
yearn to the light
is sobering
see how they turn
essence of silence:
shoots   leaves   stems
ask only for light
and turn
green tentacles
white blossoms
from day's grey drift
into bright dazzled bliss

I pray also
for the redeeming silence
no words   no thoughts
blind quiet
a touching   a searching
into the void

Deliver these ears
from voices
bondage of language
deliver me
from devious thought
a woman gone through drought
now fully whole
blessedly
complete

Let me see through
the windows

beyond

To Be Blind

To be blind
is to not-know
world's flow
is to live
so sensitive to sound
that meanings bound
     re-bound
and make non-sense

through the raw tingling
other senses
meanings fray out
there's no
concensus

To be blind
is to grope for
a   hand   an arm   a stick
sometimes a great hug
comes
and the blood hums…
but afterwards
words falter

To be blind
is to have a halter
around the neck
and friends' well-meaning
tugs
strangle one faster.

In Times Like These

Now that the trees have shed
their golden coins
upon earth's wall-to-wall
wide carpeting
we hear what the green summer
had shut out:
brute noise
the highway's decimating roar

Now that the trees
decide it's time
and time for us and squirrels
to hole up   secrete the heat

I am alone
non-person:
alive
and defying reason

I seek
(poor foiled insurgent)
belief again
in man and woman's
manifest and joined
resurgence—

Now that the trees
have laid our longing
bare...

Bellhouse Bay

Last night a full silver
moon
shone in the waters of the bay
so serene
one could believe in
an ongoing universe

And today it's summer
noon heat soaking into
arbutus trees   blackberry bushes
Today in the cities
rallies and peace demonstrations exhort

SAVE OUR WORLD   SAVE OUR CHILDREN

But save also   I say
the towhees under the blackberry bushes
eagles playing a mad caper
in the sky above Bellhouse Bay

This is not paradise
dear adam   dear eve
but it is a rung on the ladder
upwards
towards a possible
breathtaking landscape

The Prisoner Of Time

for Alan Crawley

Caught and trapped
age has put you through its mangle
I see you now, just bits and pieces
of the old flare
sparks feebly hitting
the dry air

I hear you now
an echo across the valley
JOY...LIFE...
become oyoyoy...if...
I apprehend you now
brittle chips off the old block
trying to remember a name
a place
desperate to recall
the loved face

Better to die young?
flung
from garden into ocean?
O my dear
I remember your voice dancing
its mimetic motion
I remember your keen mind
cutting through ice and stone

All I can do now
is hold your hand
all I can say
is *tovarisch tovarisch*
we are not alone.

Old Soldier

Nearing ninety, he sat on the back steps in the sun
pulling at blades of grass that poked through the cracks,
his gnarled fingers restless:
—There's been a line running through my head
verses I memorized in the third grade:

> *Soldier, rest. Thy warfare o'er*
> *sleep the sleep that knows no breaking—*

Perhaps I can find it on your bookshelf?

He seemed surprised but willing to have the search
and when the browned and spotted book was found
and opened
a four-leaf clover fell from the page he wanted.

> *The Lady of the Lake.*

I read aloud the verses
and ended where he stopped me:

> *No rude sound shall reach thine ear*
> *Armor's clang, or war-steed champing;*
> *Trump nor pibroch summon here*
> *Mustering clan, or squadron tramping.*
>
> *Yet the lark's shrill fife may come*
> *At the daybreak, from the fallow,*
> *And the bittern sound his drum,*
> *Booming from the sedgy shallow.*

—That's the bit. That's the bit
I wanted to remember.

He muttered the lines over and over.

Then as he sat there, a cloud like a hand
Moved over the face of the sun.

—Time to go in?

He stood up, jerkily. Then leaned down again
to twitch a weed from a crack in the boardwalk.

—Time *I* was pulled up, he said, offhand.

Even in These Highrises: A Suite

i

Even in these highrises
there is a crack under the door—
but no mice

She feels safe
yet unsafe
for men are predators
grandmother says
look into their history

She turns the lock
but before his knock
she unlocks it

when the door is ajar
sees only a shadow there
not the real man

Even in these highrises
fire can rage
walls can crumble

Grandmother says
there are mice waiting
around the corner

ii

Massage my back
he had urged
But how could she?
His wife had put her claws

into that flesh
Gashed he was
scarce healing
the police had told him
he couldn't go home

Then I'll massage you:
He had had about a hundred women
he explained
but the Japanese were best
they taught him how
to cherish the spine

All through
what was left of the night
he massaged her tense body
Only at morning
in perfect ease
was she ready to come

He moved away then
and stood naked at the window
his finger on the dial—
talking to his wife
on the telephone

She had loved a young man
here
in this creaky old building
with the tenant below
and his lean black dogs
dirtying the snow
outside her window

She had loved a young man
who fell from fear
he lay a-tremble
in a white fever

She fed him chicken soup
laid salve on his sores
He would be up and well
tomorrow
and leave these shores

On the airport platform
said he'd never flown
before
clung to her body
Do I have to go?

When he stumbled forward
up the runway
she felt herself pulled
as in half

But below
braced for the take-off
she found herself soaring
airborne
earth free

The Rat

Every night I talked to him
(but he paid no attention)
—Go away
leave me alone
I want to sleep
sometimes I even said please

When this didn't work
I tried tantrums
banging and screaming I hurled myself
into his corner
he would be quiet for a small while
alert, listening
but as I was falling asleep
he would start all over again
gnawing and cracking his jaws
demolishing barriers

In the end I had no reserves left
save one—
yes, poison

Not actually POISON
the label said
just a merciful
leukemia
a gasp of air at the end
a mad dash for water…

I found him, two days afterward
he hadn't quite reached the lake
unslaked

and he wasn't a rat   but
a squirrel.

Euthanasia

To leave the world
while still game for it
planting the flower garden
expecting peas   tomatoes   corn
To leave the world
where full joy seems to lie
is nonetheless happier
than to drag drag dry
into our eighties and nineties
pretending to be real
with a false leg   an aching back
teeth intractable
eyes dim
ears only half
hearing
tongue only a stutter
memory a falter

Pray pray
for all of us
that our leap into the chasm
may be agile and willing
or at least that we know
our time of going
and persuade our children
that this has to be
just so

At The Finish

The old start humming
to themselves
just to achieve belief
there *is* human sound
somewhere around

They have hope
are not afraid of dying
but of living
unable to cope

So they lie in bed longer
hugging the blankets
small children
with wool in their mouths

It takes so long
to light a fire
they hum over
the singing kettle

For these ones
no great battles
only stiff creaking knees
to be exercised
or greased

For these ones
gathering up crumbs
is a whimsical pastime
musing   forgetting

that crumbs must be thrown
out the window
for fluttering juncoes
to dance for

Strange...
birds are always hungry
yet we never see them die

Remembrance Of Things Past

For the psyche that struggled
never wept for, then
I cry now
unacknowledged

Not for this self
but for those selves
sisters:
Schumann's Clara
Mendelssohn's sister

And Anne   Charlotte   Emily
blotted out in their lifetime
by the Bells
Acton   Currer   Ellis
now outlines
shapes only
on the brick wall of history

As if an atom bomb
had always existed
poised to destroy

As if men's minds
obliterated
the minds of women
or cowed them
into submission

For that soul that struggled
feel now
only *tendresse*   tenderness

that courage to grow:
sweet seed
probed by the sun
nourished by rain
stung into protest
by the salt
tearing tongues
of the sea

Arms And The Woman

My hand within you
yours in me
by these crossed swords
we make a peace
not of this world
song without words

Towards A Love Poem

Because you elected to know me
after reading my poems
because you elected to love me
in spite of my years
I can withstand
the eyebrows lifted
the whispers of critics:
"She is so strange...."

O early morning listener
lover   explorer
who places the affirming kiss
on my vulva
catch as catch can
love in flight   weightless

I too
am learning to fly
under water

The Enchanted Isle:
A Dialogue

i

You were too busy
selling your fine pots
jars   goblets   fantastic shapes
you were too busy to see
me
standing within the shop
having chosen

But what I chose was not
the small clay jug
(held in my hand)
what I chose
was your grey hair upswept
the wrinkled skin
the crinkled lids
eyes glowing with long years of seeing
jewels set
in an earthen island

ii

I dreamed all night of you:
in my seventies' pain
your image held me
upright again

I might search for a thousand years
for my complement
yet believe time would end
that predicament

You would always be there
real as the moon

circling our island
not seventy years late
but a thousand soon

iii

We are too old to worry what we do
loving is not immoral
nor is dying.
We've succoured our young
spied out their land ahead
enough to set them flying.
Alone now in an empty house
or even coupled, in a routine yoke
a throng of us are singing
longing to soar again
open up clogged veins to further leaping
to act in unison
for our own and the island's
safekeeping

iv

Would you have lived otherwise?
Speech with another voice?
The question never arose
there was never a choice

Bewildered, we're impelled
to walk in a blindfold
take whatever turn
the hands feel out
touch tree   or rockhold—

Give credence to the heart!
Those who proceed
by logic and good sense
are withered at the start—
never achieve
old age's innocence

The Sybil

I am the one in the still
silent-seeming stream
whose centre is vortex

I am the woman
you longed to be—
and the man you challenged

the child you cherished
who was born blind
who perished

I am the teen trumpeter
defying parents—
I, too, hated
and was defeated

I am the sybil's voice
crying for knowledge:
O do not put me down
teach me to be more human

and to learn
in the clutch   of loving

how small miracles
shatter the facts—
explode!

Syzygy

"The conjunction or opposition of two heavenly bodies."

Have I lived this long
just to be finding now
my *opposite completion*?

Through snowdrifts   spring drifts
barren sand
have I lived this long
solely to know you?

Were you always there
listener   cupped ear
to all my yearnings
eyes   for my seeing
heartlifts   blotting out
despair?

Lover   brother   sister   friend
enter here
impel me forward
without fear

Bible 58, 61, 260, 80, 86, 106, 157
188,

s. now 14, 18, 76, 247, 233
205-6 ?

Book 214